DEPRESSION
Explained

DEPRESSION Explained

How you can help when someone you love is depressed

Gwendoline Smith

WITH CONTRIBUTIONS FROM
Dr Margaret Honeyman

FOREWORD BY
Professor John Werry

Email: gwendoline@gsa-ltd.co.nz
www.depressionexplained.com

First published 1996
Reprinted 1997, 2000
Second edition 2002
ISBN 0-473-08862-2

Cover painting: Ross Kinnaird
Illustrations: Bronson Yandall
Design, typesetting and production: Paradigm
Printed by Cox & Dawes

CONTENTS

In memory of my wonderful
and extraordinary father.

ACKNOWLEDGEMENTS

I'VE JUST written a book and yet I now find myself lost for words. Well, not quite. What concerns me most is finding the right words to say "thank you" to my nearest and dearest. It's not often a girl gets to go mad and come back again, and thanks to all of you my family and my dear friends and colleagues I did make it back.

To my wonderful mother Bette, for always being there.

For being special and tolerant and always believing in me, my darling Grant.

A really special thanks to two of the most wonderful psychiatric nurses ever, John and Thelma.

Another very important part of my journey back was the support and understanding of my colleagues: John Challis for gently bringing me back to work, Professor Rob Kydd for entertaining my need to stay a little bit mad, Dr Allen Fraser, to whom I am grateful for both our working relationship and his contribution to this book. I am also honoured to have a foreword by Professor John Werry.

The psychiatrist who had the most difficult task during my illness is Dr Margaret Honeyman. I don't mind admitting that I wasn't the easiest patient to treat, but I think, given the slightly unusual circumstances, you did a fantastic job and I am delighted to have your contribution to a very important chapter in my life.

I'd like to thank Jocelyn for a wonderful job, transcribing endless hours of interviews and telling me they were interesting. Thank you also to the families who gave up their time to talk to me and share their most personal thoughts.

I would also like to thank the professionals from other disciplines mentioned, for their time and interest in this project.

During the time it took to write the first edition of this book *Sharing the Load* I went to two funerals, both death by suicide. I want to acknowledge both Bill and Simon and their families. If this book can save one life, one family from that suffering, then it has served its purpose.

Thank you to young Mr Bronson Yandall for so creatively portraying my thoughts through his illustrations.

There is no book without a cover. I am ever grateful to my dear friend Diane Firth for putting her special magic into the cover for *Sharing the Load* and in 2002 gratitude to another dear friend Ross Kinnaird for putting his special touch onto the cover of *Depression Explained.*

FOREWORD

DEPRESSION is a common disorder – about one in ten persons will suffer from it to some significant degree, for several weeks or months, at least once during their lives. The risk is twice as high in women as it is in men. It produces great suffering and disability, not only to those with it, but to those who care about them. Someone once said that no physical pain is as bad as the misery of depression. Though we have had safe and effective medical treatments for depression for 30 years or more and improvements are continually occurring, large numbers of depressed people are not accessing these treatments and thus are suffering and even dying unnecessarily.

This gap between what is known and available and what the public is actually using is of major concern, and ways must be sought to bridge it. What has become apparent is that the cause of this problem lies partly in public prejudice against mental illness – especially in a pioneering, self-reliant society like New Zealand. Interestingly, when I was young, the same kind of prejudice existed against tuberculosis, which families saw as some kind of shame to be hidden from public view.

When I was training in psychiatry at McGill University in Montreal in 1960, the Canadian Mental Health Association (the equivalent of our Mental Health Foundation) adopted a slogan: 'Mental illness is like any other illness'. Sadly, we have made less progress than hoped in the intervening 35 years. The prejudice against mental illnesses like depression, and the whole concept of medical treatment for such illness, is still being fostered by sectarian groups and, sadly, some professionals. Even worse, outside medical schools, the universities and technical institutes in New Zealand are still promulgating outmoded and dangerous anti-illness and anti-medical views of psychological disorders. Media in New Zealand are equally biased against the illness view. What makes this prejudice so unfortunate is that, as this book points out, persons with mental illness need both psychological and medical treatments – not either or.

Somehow, we professionals have not found acceptable and efficient ways to sell our wares. We often speak in terms that no one understands and, despite our experience with many patients, we somehow lack the essential empathic component to get people to hear the message. Over the past few years, there has been a shift in emphasis away from professional-driven to consumer-based methods of public education. Prominent persons such as Spike Milligan, Rod Steiger and Michael Dukakis are more frequently speaking in public and writing of their own battle with depression. But it is not only the patients who are forthcoming. Families also suffer and, over the last few years, some of our political leaders have spoken of the stress and grief that depression has caused for all members of the family, not just those affected.

Now Gwendoline has used her experience as a psychologist, a writer and media expert, and a patient, to write a book to help other sufferers and their loved ones overcome ignorance, fear and prejudice to access what is their right – the best in treatment and care that the country can afford. This is a down-to-earth book with a very clear audience and well-defined objectives. I found it clear, practical, funny, informative, compassionate and riveting. I have checked it out and can say that it is factually accurate. I am sure that those for whom it is written will find it helpful, but professionals, too, would benefit from reading it and get a better insight into the patient's and family's view of things.

I have worked with Gwendoline in Auckland-based hospitals, and I knew her first as a likeable, colourful person and admirable colleague, highly respected by nursing and medical staff for her clinical abilities, with a remarkable ability to cut through the fog and lay things bare. When she came to me as she was just beginning to recover from her depression, I could not believe it was the same person – all the stuffing seemed to have been knocked out of her – gone was her mordant wit, her colourful dress and lust for life. She went on to speak of her illness and what she had learned from it.

More importantly, she also spoke of her determination to help those like herself and her family, who had suffered directly or indirectly, had been afflicted by prejudice and ignorance about mental illness and had not known what to do or whether to accept treatment early when it was first offered. To achieve this objective she intended to use her skills and write a personalised book, since she felt, correctly, that this would add cogency and acceptability to her message for those who most needed to hear it. I admired her courage and encouraged her to go ahead. I would like congratulate Random House for accepting her proposal for the original manuscript.

As they say in New Zealand, you can't keep a good man (woman) down!

John S. Werry MD
Emeritus Professor of Psychiatry
University of Auckland

INTRODUCTION

I'M GOING to start by working on the assumption that if you've been drawn to a book such as this, you are concerned and distressed about someone you love. You suspect or have had it medically confirmed that they are suffering from depression. But you don't seem to be able to fully understand what they are going through and, most of the time, you don't know if what you are doing is for the best. Sometimes, you may even feel angry and frustrated, but most of all you feel helpless, surrounded by well-meaning advice and varying expert opinions, and yet still not knowing which way to turn. *Depression Explained* is a book written for you, for the families and loved ones of those suffering from depression.

When I first approached Random House with my initial proposal, I was determined to avoid any form of personal disclosure. In fact, my exact words were, "I'm not interested in this book as a vehicle for self-indulgent catharsis. You go to therapists for treatment, not publishers." I still feel very strongly about the issue of self-indulgence, as I see it often in contemporary self-help literature.

However, the more I thought about it and spoke to other people, friends and clients, it did occur to me that what is unique about my situation is that I am able to bring you the knowledge of an academic and health professional as well as the insight of my own experience. Far from being a book that was conceived on the fifth floor of an ivory tower, it was being created as I sat across the desk from my psychiatrist, as I lay in bed staring at the ceiling, as I walked into the chemist and handed over my prescription for anti-psychotic medication.

Once I had recovered and was able to talk reflectively about what had happened, I got a real sense of how difficult it had been for my friends and family and how little they understood of what had been going on. (Those friends, of course, who weren't other mental health professionals.) It was obvious to them that something was wrong, but what should they do? Should they get involved or wait for me to reach out to them? What sort of support did I need and how could they best offer that support? Friends became concerned with issues of privacy. They knew my family was involved and didn't want to interfere.

But my family, on the other hand, had never dealt with psychiatric illness before and they themselves were battling with what to do for the best. They were facing decisions of whether or not I needed to be committed to a psychiatric institution, versus trying to protect my career and public profile from the stigma that surrounds psychiatric illness. Essentially, they faced many of the things that you are currently dealing with. It has been the acknowledgement of those difficulties that I have recognised in writing this book. The intention is to ease your burden, and make this very difficult time a little bit easier.

First, I would like to tell you a little of what it feels like from the inside. Because when someone is suffering from depression, that is almost impossible to articulate. For they don't really understand it themselves – all they know is that they feel emotionally disabled and unable to communicate with anybody, no matter where you fit in their lives. It's not you whom they have stopped loving, it's life. Put it this way. I'm a busy professional person – I write, I work on radio and television, I lecture at universities, run seminars for corporations – in essence, I am a communicator. I make a living talking to people. When I'm not getting paid for it, I'm still doing it because I love to be with people. There's nothing I like better than sitting around a sturdy dinner table, with plenty to eat, plenty to drink, and lots and lots of conversation, debate, wit, humour. It stimulates and enriches my life. Yet, when I was depressed, there was no colour in anything. I couldn't digest food, let alone prepare a dinner party. I couldn't even converse with people, not even those closest to me.

I had become depressed after a manic episode, during which I had lived as the Second Messiah for nearly a month. As you can imagine, there was a lot to be done, saving the planet being no small task at the best of times. Travelling through space and time, absorbing Stephen Hawking's metaphysical theories as though they were written as a script for *Sesame Street*, I was having a wonderful and exhilarating time. (As a very dear colleague of mine once said, "if you could bottle mania as a designer drug, you'd make a fortune.") I must admit, though, being guided through the day by numerological interpretations of car licence-plate numbers tended to confuse things at times. Team that up with the delusion that I was Elizabeth Taylor's first daughter, the result of a torrid affair with Walt Disney, at the same time believing Richard Burton was my father, but questioning whether either of them were in fact my father, given that I was immaculately conceived. The only question of any relevance being, "When will she agree to take medication?" My answer to that: "I don't recall reading anywhere that Jesus was prescribed lithium." …I think you're starting to get the picture. Yes, I was mad.

The only problem was that when you're so high for so long, eventually you're going to have to come back down to earth. And, having used up all my mental energy flying around re-existing, re-birthing and being re-incarnated in Ancient Egypt, I didn't just land, I crashed. Initially, I put my flat mood and lack of enthusiasm down to the anti-psychotic medication I had been prescribed. Which wouldn't have been totally out of the question – you could put a wounded bull elephant to sleep with that stuff. But much to my disgust there was more to it than that. I was becoming depressed. I tried with all my will and the energy I had left to fight it on my own, but I just couldn't do it. So it was back to the psychiatrist, and back to the drug cupboard.

I had developed another inconvenient little condition, known in the industry as 'post-psychotic depression'. This particular ailment was to put me off work for another six months, not to mention the disappearance of any semblance of a social life. I was officially in bed and clinically depressed. I remember trying desperately to sleep until ten or eleven in the morning, because I was terrified of how difficult it was going to be trying to cope if the day was any longer.

I once attended the funeral of a very dear man who had unsuccessfully battled with depression. In one of the eulogies, depression had been described as: "The illness where it always feels like three o'clock in the morning and you are the only one awake." If you can imagine how that feels every waking hour, you're getting close. Depression flattens you like a steamroller – on the way through it smashes your self-esteem, your confidence, it smashes you. I felt that I would never work again, never be able to laugh again or chat and pass the time just talking about not much at all.

I remember when I first started to go out of the house. I was at a girlfriend's birthday party one evening and I learned a trick of parroting conversations. I would listen and attempt to memorise a topic of discussion on one side of the room, then move across the room to another group of people, and when there was an opportune moment I would repeat the conversation. This enabled me at least to participate in what was going on around me. I had never felt so disabled, so paralysed by my own fears and anxiety.

Only able to observe the world, I would try to warm myself by being close to the sound of someone's laughter, but as soon as it had gone, the room was once again dark and cold. As a clinician I had often witnessed the pain on the faces of my clients, but never before had I been able to come close to understanding the degree of debilitation, the intensity of their despair. (Not that I'm recommending it as a compulsory training experience for budding psychotherapists.)

Looking back, the worst part is that you don't know when it will end or if it ever will. It just seems to go on and on, week after week, for some people month after month if they do not respond immediately to treatment. Fortunately, in my case, my physiology welcomed the first anti-depressants I was prescribed. It was the longest five weeks of my life, but when the medication started to kick in, I could feel little bits of myself returning. My psychotherapist encouraged me to grab hold of the smallest changes and acknowledge them.

My diary read:

"It's been a long time since I've retched over food.
Stopped my sleeping medication, worried about dependency.
My psychiatrist thought I was looking better.
Had a social conversation."

One week later:

"I'm still able to hold down food.
Cooked a meal.
A friend commented that my eyes had started to come alive."

I was so used to measuring my accomplishments by articles published, business deals negotiated, projects completed, I found it very difficult to revel in the absence of nausea, but then I didn't have a choice. Eventually, I could feel that I was back, not quite the same – a lot slower, but there. Not that one could realistically expect to go mad, astral travel, thrash about in Jung's 'collective subconscious' and make it back exactly the same. In fact, it would have to be one of the most profound experiences of my life. Upon saying that, it was also frightening, particularly as I started to realise the enormity of what had happened. With my own mind as the vehicle, I had travelled the depths of my consciousness. At times I felt moved by a great sense of spiritual awareness and, at other times, it was as though I held the key to the miracles of DNA. Then there were the times when I just felt desperately alone with no sense of reason, no sense of meaning

But, like I said, "I made it back" and there are a lot of things I'm grateful for. Most of all, I'm grateful that I made it through a very difficult time in my life, that I was treated successfully by means of modern psychiatry, that for me it was a psychotic episode and I don't live with an illness every day, as others do. But, I do recall how it felt to live with the stigma that accompanies psychiatric illness, albeit for only a relatively short period in my life. I also remember, with at times painful clarity the helplessness of my family. It is these memories that bring me to 'the why of the book'.

THE WHY OF THE BOOK

During the last session with my psychotherapist, Anne recorded the following comment: "Gwendoline hopes to pursue long-term career dream of giving psychiatry a better public image." This isn't with the intention of lobbying for an increase in hourly rates for psychiatrists – they get paid more than psychologists as it stands. The emphasis is on 'destigmatising' psychiatric illness.

If psychiatry is brought out of the Dark Ages, and psychiatric treatment finally terminates its relationship with Nurse Ratchet and Jack Nicholson in *One Flew Over the Cuckoo's Nest*, it will be much easier for individuals and their families to seek help. And it will become easier for those same individuals to be treated for an illness without the fear of being ostracised as though they were carrying a highly infectious disease. The prejudices that surround psychiatric ill-health are, of course, the result of fear and ignorance, and the best way to overcome them is through education

It is the need for education and the sharing of knowledge and experience that brings me to the main purpose of the book – 'demystification'. Being close to someone who is suffering is very difficult and stressful. However, a lot of fears and anxieties also stem from a lack of knowledge and understanding – not knowing what to do and if what you are doing is of any help. A sense of being completely alone with it all.

I have written *Depression Explained* to provide you with information, based on current research into the treatment of depression, that will hopefully allay some of those fears and, most importantly, give you access to the stories of others who have been exactly where you are. Self-identification enables you to learn ways of coping from the experiences of others. That, I believe, is one of the most potent remedies for you right now.

THE HOW OF THE BOOK

I have composed the content of this book in a manner designed to be 'user friendly'. Each chapter can be read individually, like a magazine article. You may wish to go directly to the chapter that most specifically relates to your situation. However, the thing to be aware of is that although there are numerous causes of depression, there is a commonality of symptoms, along with very definite themes about how people behave and feel when they are depressed. There are also similarities in the responses of friends and families, despite the age, gender, or different diagnostic evaluations of the person with depression. So within each chapter there is something to be gleaned, something to relate to and learn from.

There is also information to help you discern where best to seek help – the differing types of help available and what they have to offer. Depression affects judgement and, hence, it may be left up to you to decide not only where to go for help but whether or not the chosen intervention is of any benefit.

There are components of the book that are very factual and will provide you with knowledge regarding the physiology of depression and how pharmacology works.

As I mentioned earlier, this is a book for the loved ones, the nearest and dearest, it is not a self-help book for the person with depression. However, you may find it very helpful to chat to your loved one about what you are learning as you go through. This may give you a closer understanding of how he or she is feeling day by day, and help maintain ongoing communication where possible.

No matter how much you love someone, being with a person who is depressed is very draining. You need to take care of yourself – reading *Depression Explained* could be your first step in doing that.

CHAPTER 1

What it is, Why it is, & How to Spot it

ALTHOUGH a number of you may have already sought medical advice and have had the depressive illness diagnosed, some of you may still be trying to determine whether or not your loved one is depressed, or for that matter what depression is. You may have noticed certain changes in your loved one's moods and behaviour, but when you imply that there may be something wrong and suggest a visit to the doctor, you are met with resistance and denial. The most important thing at this junction is that you do not take his or her often hostile responses personally and that you continue to research your concerns. The first step in this process is some basic understanding of what depression is and how to recognise the symptoms.

Depression is one of those words that has managed to sneak out of the medical dictionaries into everyday usage. A typical example would be: you bump into someone you know on the street one day, and out of politeness ask them how they are. To which they reply:

> *"Oh, God I'm depressed, I woke up this morning, it was a beautiful day, I was feeling great, only to have some jerk run into the back of my car, which pushed me into the back of the car in front of me, which just happened to be my boss's wife and now she's in hospital with whiplash, and they were about to go on holiday, because it was their wedding anniversary and I just feel like killing myself!"*

This is an example of somebody having an exceptionally bad day. The word 'depressed' is used to describe feeling down and stressed.

We also use the word 'depressed to describe the feelings of sadness and grief we may be experiencing after a personal tragedy or loss. These feelings are, of course, appropriate and natural, and there would be more reason for concern if a person was not able to express himself emotionally. However, if these feelings become overwhelming and unmanageable, it could be because the individual is 'clinically' depressed. Depression in this context refers to the illness. The guidelines on the following page will help you determine the difference.

SYMPTOMS OF DEPRESSION

1. **Loss of interest or pleasure in all activities once enjoyed.**
2. **Changes in weight or appetite (either significant weight gain or weight loss).**
3. **Changes in sleeping patterns (restless sleep, unable to sleep, early morning wakening, sleeping too much, feeling more depressed in the morning).**
4. **Fatigue or loss of energy.**
5. **Feeling hopeless or worthless. Loss of self-confidence.**
6. **Irrational thinking (beliefs not based on reality, preoccupation with physical disease, constant feelings of inappropriate guilt).**
7. **Inability to concentrate, remember things, or make decisions.**
8. **Ongoing thoughts of death or suicide (wishing to die, or attempts at suicide).**
9. **Loss of sexual drive.**
10. **Feelings of sadness or irritability.**
11. **Restlessness or decreased activity, boredom.**

Note: As a loved one looking in from the outside you may also notice changes in physical appearance. Your loved one may become less interested in the way he dresses, how he presents himself, walking with a bowed stance or slouching. He may lack expression when talking with you and it may seem that talking has become a great effort.
Not all of these symptoms are necessary. However, if you observe four or more of these symptoms for a period of longer than two weeks you should seek professional help.

People can become depressed for all sorts of reasons and at all different stages of their lives. Current research provides us with more information on childhood and adolescent depression, perhaps previously undetected because it was seen in terms of developmental stages – "Oh, it's just a phase." With the elderly, memory impairment, lack of drive and motivation, slowed speech or movement may have been misdiagnosed as senility or even the effects of a mild stroke.

It is also obvious that many of the symptoms are seen in physical illness and your doctor, if not properly trained, may focus solely on that possibility, ignoring depression.

It is rare that a single reason can be pinpointed as the cause of depression. It tends to be the result of various contributing factors. One or more of the following factors could apply, and these are interrelated.

Known Causes

1. HEREDITARY

Research has clearly demonstrated the existence of a genetic predisposition towards depression, in the same way that other illnesses, for example, heart disease and duodenal ulcers, tend to be hereditary. This doesn't necessarily meant that if one of your parents has suffered from a depressive illness, you will automatically suffer also. It means that you are more likely to (15-25 per cent risk), that your genetic capacity to tolerate stress is less, and hence the risk is increased.

2. BIOCHEMICAL

What has become increasingly evident with the explosion of knowledge about the functioning of the brain is that mood is mediated by electrical activity and certain chemicals within the brain. It is understood that high levels of stress can lead to chemical imbalance and lower the functioning of and effectiveness of certain activities in the brain, resulting in mood imbalance. Scientists have gleaned vital information in this area through studying the effects of drugs that affect depression, such as antidepressants and lithium. The observable changes in brain chemistry in response to these medications have generated theories about the differences in brain chemistry of people with and without depressive illness.

3. PHYSICAL

Depression can often accompany physical illness, especially those that are life-threatening. Strokes and head injuries also need to be accounted for. There are instances where depression can follow illnesses that change the immune system, such as influenza and glandular fever. Any physical examination should also check for abnormalities such as under-activity of the thyroid gland, or the existence of liver disease, such as hepatitis.

Gross vitamin and iron deficiencies in the diet are known to produce depression, which is relieved through dietary correction. Individuals claim great benefits from moderating and restricting diet. However, research in this area is difficult to substantiate.

Attention is also being paid to the phenomenon of the seasonality of depression (seasonal affective disorder). Research suggests that various biological factors may be critically affected by the climatic environment, especially the length of daylight.

A prior history of depression increases the possibility of a further episode by an estimated 50%. Alcohol- and drug-abuse will also increase biological risk.

In the case of manic depressive illness or hypomanic episodes, depression is considered to be an expected eventual outcome – though it may not happen until after several manic episodes.

4. ANXIETY

As research has developed the link between anxiety and depression has become increasingly more apparent. People can often experience symptoms of both simultaneously. Individuals with high 'trait' anxiety, ie. where the overall level of anxiety is consistently high, the more anxious they will become when stressed. Individuals with this high trait anxiety have been shown to be more vulnerable to the onset of depression.

Depressive symptoms can also co-present with the range of anxiety disorders including panic, social phobia, obsessive – compulsive disorder and post-traumatic stress. Many of the symptoms associated with depression and anxiety, such as unrealistic worrying, feelings of panic, apprehension and fear, sleeplessness, irritability and fatigue will overlap. Because of these similarities accurate diagnosis is often difficult. It is not uncommon for doctors to focus on and treat only one disorder. They will tend to treat what they perceive to be the primary problem.

It is also very common for people to become highly anxious in the early stages of depression, as a result the doctor may treat the anxiety and overlook the depression. Likewise it is common for people with long-term anxiety disorders to become depressed. As you can see, it is essential that there is an accurate diagnosis, to ensure the effectiveness of the treatment. This is the case with both medications and psychotherapy, the treatment approaches have differences. The newer medications SSRI's (selective serotonin reuptake inhibitors) and in particular the SNRI's (serotonin-noradrenaline reuptake inhibitor) have begun to address the complex relationship between anxiety and depression. For these specialised differences, this can be where a referral to a psychiatrist from your doctor can prove to make a very valuable contribution.

5. PSYCHOLOGICAL

It is especially important to be able to identify psychological factors in the treatment of depression. Someone with a purely biological depression that responds well to medication may require no other form of intervention. If the origins of the depression are as a result of psychological stressors, these must be addressed separately.

Psychological theories of depression tend to be based on the premise that early childhood trauma, such as the loss of parents, or unsettled chaotic and abusive environments can lead to depression later on in life. However, only a relatively small percentage of individuals exposed to such early life experiences in fact develop depression, once again raising the issue of genetic predisposition.

Certain personality types seem to be more prone to depressive illness, for instance, people who find it difficult to adjust to change and are inflexible in their approach to life, and individuals who are very dependent on others for their well-being (as in the case of the elderly).

There is also increasing evidence to illustrate the relationship between temperament and depression, showing the tendencies of certain individuals to react more negatively to stress. Their response will often involve far more negative thinking when interpreting life events.

6. LEARNED HELPLESSNESS

This is a psychological approach formulated by the clinician and researcher M.P. Seligman, based on the notion that if humans are repeatedly exposed to unpleasant, uncontrollable events, they learn that trying to change things is a waste of time. They lose their motivation and sense of optimism, feeling increasingly helpless and depressed.

7. SOCIAL

Research has shown that an excess of stressful life events can lead to depression. A leading researcher in this area, Dr Eugene Paykel, has found that the risk of developing depression rises six-fold in people experiencing such highly stressful events as bereavement, financial disaster or loss of a job. This is especially the case at certain stages of life where individuals are more vulnerable, such as childbirth and menopause in women and retirement in men.

Other social risk factors include social disadvantage (eg. poverty, unemployment). Family discord such as conflict, poor parenting, child abuse and neglect. Inadequate social networks, being isolated from friends and family, perhaps as a result of caring for an elderly parent or someone with a chronic illness (depression can be included in this category).

8. GENDER

Studies show that twice as many women become depressed as men. Reasons for this phenomenon include biological (hormonal) and social factors. Women's conditioning encourages them to turn inwards when faced with difficulties; men are encouraged to express themselves outwardly by taking action and this may be through anger. Seligman also suggests that the 'pursuit of thinness' in our culture has a lot to answer for, especially with regards depression and eating disorders. However, biology is also a factor. Recent studies have shown that at puberty, as testosterone levels rise, boys become less and less confiding and more independent of people, which may protect them against depression.

In conclusion, nobody knows the exact cause of depression. What does seem highly likely is that there is no one single cause – that the forces of both nature and nurture are in operation. The details of the ratio, or 'what came first, the chicken or the egg?' will undoubtedly remain part of the academic pursuit for the definitive treatment. In the meantime, we will go with what we have. The following chapters will introduce you to some of the treatment options available, and the current consensus, as well as my personal and professional experience of their effectiveness.

CHAPTER 2

Images of Psychiatry

AFTER my depression had been treated and I was working again, I was far more aware of people's responses to the mention of seeking psychiatric help. One day I was sitting with a client, listening to her story of personal betrayal, bankruptcy, sleepless nights, stress, tearfulness, thoughts of suicide. As her story unfolded she had the full house of depressive symptoms. I gently suggested that I would like her to see a psychiatrist to be assessed for some antidepressant medication. She clutched her handkerchief, began sobbing and cried out, "Oh God, I'm not that bad am I?"

I remembered only too well how that felt. I was sitting in Margaret's (my psychiatrist) office one afternoon for my fortnightly check-up. I was notably thinner, unable to be on my own, anxious, tearful – in fact, looking back, I too had the full house of symptoms, but I didn't want to admit that I was depressed. I had to sort this for myself – I was going to positive think my way out of it, and besides, what was a pill going to do? I didn't need any more drugs. Margaret pointed out to me that she had given me long enough to get well on my own, that I was the patient here, and that in her medical opinion I was depressed and required antidepressant medication. I put my head in my hands and sobbed. I felt that I had failed.

But why? Why should I have felt that way? After all, depression is an illness, like any other, so you go to a doctor and have it treated. It seems simple enough, but for a myriad of reasons it isn't. People have an almost inherent mistrust of psychiatry, some of which may be due to negative experiences within their own family, but for the most part is a direct result of the mythology and misconceptions that surround psychiatric medicine. What we now commonly refer to as the stigma associated with mental illness.

The aim of this chapter is to provide you with knowledge and understanding that will help you to feel less anxious about forms of psychiatric treatment, and more able to participate in the decision-making process.

Also, if your loved one is in denial or refusing to seek help, it may help you understand why she is feeling that way, and perhaps encourage her to see things differently. Because the really crazy thing about all of this is that biological treatments for depression do usually work. It is accepted that approximately 80 per cent of people suffering from major depression will respond to one of the antidepressant drugs, either on its own or in combination. Yet in the same way I had felt, your loved one, and perhaps you yourself, may feel, that going to a psychiatrist and taking a pill is the absolute last resort.

Given what a hellishly difficult patient I was, who better to advise on these issues and perhaps dispel a few myths than my own psychiatrist? I first asked Margaret what she thought about the widespread resistance to seeking psychiatric consultation.

MARGARET: I think that some individuals don't know quite why they have even been referred to a psychiatrist and there's an underlying resistance and resentment, which is obviously not a good start.

GWENDOLINE: I guess some of that has to do with the fact that people aren't quite sure what psychiatrists actually do. I wish I had a dollar for every time someone has said to me, "Oh, so you're a psychologist, not a psychiatrist. So, what's the difference?" I explain to them that the main difference is that psychiatrists are trained medically and, as doctors, focus on the definite signs and symptoms of the illness, to formulate a diagnosis and decide whether or not to treat it biologically. Psychiatrists are able to prescribe medication. Psychologists focus primarily on the psychological and emotional issues, such as conflicts at home, financial problems, and pressures arising from environmental sources.

MARGARET: Yes, that's true, but I also think it has to do with how you suggest it to people. Being sent to a psychiatrist by your family doctor is seen as the end of the road. This really truly means "I'm losing it, I'm crackers, I'm stark raving mad." I try to frame it for them in terms of having a depressive illness and that going to see a psychiatrist is going to see a doctor who specialises in these illnesses. I think if you just say, "I want you to see a psychiatrist," people do respond very badly – it's like saying 'funeral director' – it's socially unacceptable.

GWENDOLINE: I suppose that has to do with the stigma attached to the illness. It's as though people still see it as a flaw in their character, a lack of moral fibre. Because of that, people try to hide it, like it is something to be ashamed of.

MARGARET: Yes, I think undoubtedly that's part of it. We talk about society's stigma, but it's usually the individual's own sense of stigma or sense of failure that is the concept that needs to be corrected. In my experience, even the families are far more encouraging of the step to see a psychiatrist than the individual is themselves. There may be the odd occasion when family members have said, "Oh, you don't want to go and see somebody like that, they'll just mess up your head," but more often the friends and family want them to get some help, and the individual resists.

GWENDOLINE: Do you think resistance is connected to the perception of the relationship between psychiatry and drug therapy?

MARGARET: That is often the case. People think that they will be turned into a zombie. Part of it is also the fear that they are going to be sent away to an institution for a lengthy period of time. The other thing they begin to fear is that if they have to see a psychiatrist and take drugs, they've got something incurable. I don't think that the public by and large would have much idea of there being a range of very curable psychiatric disorders.

Just the other day, I was giving evidence on behalf of a woman who had a puerperal psychosis (a severe but rare form of post-natal depression). I found the questions of counsel quite distressing in that they inferred it was an ongoing condition that would always affect her judgement and mothering skills. It was a great challenge to make it clear that it had remitted completely – that it is an illness that does remit completely.

GWENDOLINE: In reflection, it has been very important to have depression explained to me in terms of a medical model (ie. an illness). It meant that it wasn't to do with a flaw in my personality or that I was too weak to 'pull myself together'. But at the time, I remember fighting you all the way, and I know I'm not the only person guilty of that. Why do you think we have those feelings, Margaret, is it because it's our brain you're about to 'tamper' with? Fears of the mind police?

MARGARET: People do have the viewpoint that somehow the spirit is encompassed in the mind or the brain and whilst this may or may not be true depending on your philosophical stance, it still boils down to having a brain that's working efficiently. The other aspect is that the brain does control all other functions of the body and if it is perceived as the control centre, we are even more reluctant to admit that there might be something wrong with it.

It's important to know that the brain's just another organ of your body. It's a very specialised one and central to the rest of your functioning, but *it is just another organ of your body* and things can go wrong with it the same as they can with your liver, your stomach, your pancreas. We accept that these organs may have problems that respond to medication, and the brain is no different. We do not expect to be able to pull ourselves together and make it better if we've just had a heart attack. It's not a question of moral strength or weakness as some people seem to believe.

GWENDOLINE: I can really identify with the comments you have made about our perceptions of the function of the brain. Because our eyes, ears and breathing apparatus are attached to our heads, and we think by using our brain, which is inside our head, we cannot help but feel that we live in our heads.

> As a result of this we tend to credit the brain with all sorts of mystical powers, and become very protective and suspicious of any suggested treatments. At closer inspection, the bulk of this suspicion comes from the images we have of psychiatry.

Everybody has at least one story of macabre and cruel treatment. Have you heard the one about the prominent 30-year-old attorney from Vermont who was treated for depression by having his head held down in a bucket of water? He drowned before they successfully treated the depression. It's a true story, but people forget to mention that it happened in 1806, at the same time as medics were using leeches and other bizarre medical treatments.

The Citizens Commission on Human Rights, established by the Church of Scientology, will still, in response to a phone call, provide you with articles entitled, for example, 'Psychiatry causes Brain Damage', with helpful descriptions of the "application of hog-slaughtering skills to humans, creating one of the most brutal techniques of psychiatry" (referring to electroconvulsive therapy – ECT).

These images are perpetuated by film and television, in fact the media at large. The blatant misuse of ECT and lobotomy to control anti-social behaviour, in *One Flew Over the Cuckoo's Nest* as recently as the 1970s, did nothing to ease the fears or warm the lay person to psychiatric treatments. Although a delightful and entertaining character, Frasier, the psychiatrist/analyst in the American sitcom *Cheers*, is portrayed as being far more 'dysfunctional' than any of his prospective clients. In a recent film release, *Mr Jones*, Richard Gere plays a manic-depressive. His psychiatrist immediately falls in love with him and wants to throw away her career. Woody Allen spends his adult life making movies about his time in psychoanalysis and how much it cost him, and then runs away with his step-daughter. I rest my case.

As long as these perceptions of psychiatric practice endure, millions of people worldwide remain untreated as a result of fear and ignorance, based on outdated images of psychiatry. Even with all my experience as a health professional I felt frightened. This next chapter is designed to give you some insight into the contemporary *reality* of psychiatric treatment. The perception may be that psychiatrists are 'shrinks' – the next best thing to a witch doctor – the reality is... psychiatrists are doctors, too.

CHAPTER 3

Psychiatrists are Doctors, Too

THE primary role of the psychiatrist is the medical diagnosis and treatment of psychiatric ill-health. Their particular, but not exclusive, emphasis is on biological treatment. Your family doctor is able to prescribe only some antidepressant medications and, in fact, most people presenting with depression are treated successfully by their own doctor. Psychiatrists, however, are the specialists in this area, in the same way that oncologists specialise in treating cancer.

The initial focus of a psychiatric evaluation needs to be on determining whether someone has a biochemical or a psychologically based depression. A skilled psychiatrist would be able to differentiate between the two and, hence, make an informed prediction about the helpfulness of biological treatments (medication, ECT), psychological therapies, or a combination of both. The following are the questions that I needed answered to allay my fears of the biological treatments, in particular drug therapy.

GWENDOLINE: I don't know if you remember, Margaret, but I was determined to fight the depression on my own and really didn't want to have to take drugs. Can people overcome it on their own, or are drugs always necessary?

MARGARET: By the time people come for a psychiatric consultation they have been trying on their own for some time without success.

Often it hasn't worked because there is a chemical imbalance, which requires medication to correct.

Certain individuals may be able to feel much better and quite positive for periods of time if they focus on some distraction, perhaps interact with friends, or quote "think positively", but this cannot be sustained and the depressive feelings return as soon as the activity is stopped.

I often use the analogy of the refrigerated room where the thermostat is set to cold. If we concentrate on imagining hot sun shining on our bodies, we may feel slightly warmer as long as we concentrate intently. But as soon as we stop the positive imagery, we realise we are still cold. Likewise, we may jump up and down for five minutes being very busy, but as soon as we stop the activity, the feelings of being cold return.

GWENDOLINE: Is it true, though, that in many instances depressive illness will naturally remit?

MARGARET: Yes, after a period of some months, say 6-24 months, it may go away.

GWENDOLINE: Knowing what it's like, I can't imagine ever encouraging anyone to suffer that long.

MARGARET: Exactly. Why tolerate many months of painful ill health when there may be relief in a few weeks. Psychic pain is as intolerable as any physical pain. The problem for the sufferer is that no one can see it, there is no blood, nothing tangible to validate the feelings.

GWENDOLINE: I always thought that taking drugs was just a way of avoiding reality and avoiding facing how you feel. After all, they can't change situations.

MARGARET: That's true, but they may alter one's ability to cope with circumstances. Problems may seem to be less overwhelming and problem-solving abilities may be restored to normal. Medication may also restore the ability to experience emotions at a normal level. You can still feel sadness and happiness, rather than all your emotions being on the depressed side of the scale.

Antidepressants are not drugs of addiction or dependence, in that you don't require increasing doses to attain the same relief, and there are not usually withdrawal effects when you come off them. Although I strongly advise that this is monitored by your doctor or treating psychiatrist. A small number of people may have a recurrence of symptoms after stopping the medication and might need to remain on treatment for a longer period. A very small number of people appear to require long-term maintenance treatment.

GWENDOLINE: Now, I know there are different types of anti-depressants. Can you explain something of what they are and how they work.

MARGARET: There are a range of different medications that have been found to be effective in treating depressive illness. Some have been in use for 30 years, such as the monoamine oxidase inhibitors (MAOIs) and the tricyclics. Others have been researched and developed over the last several years. These are the selective serotonin reuptake inhibitors (SSRIs), these include Prozac, Paxil and Cipramil, and the serotonin-noradrenalin reuptake inhibitors (SNRI's) such as Venlafaxine XR (working with both serotonin and noradrenalin). They have been found to be just as effective in treating depression as the tricyclics, but have a much gentler side effect profile, and also have a safety factor in that they are extremely difficult for patients to overdose on. These new generation anti-depressants are also making a significant contribution, particularly in cases where there are high levels of anxiety associated with the depression. We refer to this as co-morbid mood and anxiety disorder and although there maybe a common underlying cause, manage-ment of both is essential for successful treatment. As we learn more about the relationship between anxiety and depression, these newer drugs will play an ever-increasing role.

These groups of antidepressants act in different ways, but all have the effect of modifying the levels of chemicals or neurotrans-mitters in the brain. These neurotransmitters are sometimes called 'chemical messengers' and are the agents by which information is transferred from one nerve or brain cell to another. In this case, the data that is transferred relates to the maintenance of normal mood levels. If there is an imbalance in the level of chemicals, say a slight shortage, then depression may be the result. This can be treated by one of these drugs, which act to improve the amount of the neurotransmitter available to the brain, possibly by improving the 'recycling' of the chemical, preventing its breakdown or by altering the uptake.

The two main neurotransmitters involved in depressive disorders are serotonin and noradrenaline. Some antidepressants are more effective on one system rather than another, some act on both, and some are quite selective. Unfortunately, we don't have a means of telling diagnostically which system in the patient is most out of order and so, occasionally, more than one drug may have to be tried before an effective treatment is achieved. Sometimes a combination of drugs may be required.

The amount that's prescribed is also something that to a certain extent is tailored to the individual but it's largely determined by the dosage that's known to be required for a cure.

GWENDOLINE: How long do people have to take them for? Do you need to be on them for life?

MARGARET: The majority of people would be on treatment with antidepressants for about six to nine months, but obviously the period of time can vary a lot according to the individual and circumstances. For instance, one would not recommend stopping the medication after six months if the individual had just gone through a divorce, moved house or had their cat put down.

GWENDOLINE: I'd like to add something to that list, Margaret: anniversaries. The anniversary of a death, significant loss, or some other traumatic event is a very vulnerable time for people. Memories are very powerful things and they can greatly influence the way we feel. So, if your loved one is thinking of discussing with his doctor the discontinuation of his medication, check that there are no unpleasant anniversaries just around the corner.

On the other hand, say there was nothing like that, and your loved one had been feeling really good for quite a while, would it then be appropriate to stop medication?

MARGARET: People will usually feel considerably better after a few weeks and question the need to continue. I explain to people that the period of time on medication with normal neurotransmitter levels being maintained by the drugs allows the brain to recover its own ability to maintain normal neurotransmitter levels. It appears to take at least several months for this to happen.

Again, it's helpful to use a medical analogy. If you have a really debilitating illness like glandular fever, you may feel you have recovered until you start to exert yourself. You then realise that you need an extended period of convalescence to recover completely and that it does take some time to resolve.

GWENDOLINE: What you've just said reminds me of a couple of really important things that I learned along the way. First was the realisation that the medication was, in fact, a *course*, and that feeling better wasn't the signal to stop taking it. It's useful to see it in the same way as antibiotics: the course has to be completed.

In fact when clients say to me, *"I think I'll stop taking my medication now. I don't like to take drugs and I'm feeling so much better"*, my standard and very **assertive** reply goes something like this: ***"the reason you feel you don't need them is because you are taking them"***.

Convalescence was the other thing I wanted to mention. Recovering from depression really does take time. Your loved one has felt like such a burden for so long that she wants to get back into life, doing things, helping around the house, firing on all cylinders again. That's not how it works and you will probably need to remind them: "The brain is just another organ of your body, if you'd torn your ligaments running a triathlon, you wouldn't sign up and start training for another one as soon as you could walk again."

The other aspect that we need to cover, Margaret, is the expectations. When can you expect the medication to work?

MARGARET: It is often frustrating at the start of treatment to be expecting a dramatic relief of the depressive feelings and symptoms and to find that nothing seems to happen for quite a while. This is because most of these drugs take some time to build up in the brain and produce the desired effect. This delay can seem intolerable, and patience is required during this phase. It may take from one to six weeks for the effect, but the usual pattern is of some lifting of mood to take place in 10 to 20 days.

Most people seem to feel that they experience an easing of the pain and distress quite early on, although it takes a week or two longer to start to feel that the depression's actually lifting.

GWENDOLINE: I believe that to be a very important understanding for everybody involved. Because if you expect the drugs to work immediately and they don't, it's very easy to set yourself up to lose hope that anything will work, and all of those fears of *"What if they don't work?"* start to emerge.

MARGARET: Just in response to that, it is quite possible that the first drug won't work. We know that roughly 70 per cent of people will respond to the first drug tried, and most of the others will respond to one of the other antidepressants available. Unfortunately, we can't do specific laboratory tests to know exactly which drug will suit each individual best.

This can be a very difficult phase of treatment because of the patient's anxiety and doubts about the effectiveness of treatment. It is important to sustain patience and hope.

GWENDOLINE: Can other people tell that someone is on antidepressants?

MARGARET: No, other people can't tell, unless the medication is not suiting the individual, in which case there might be noticeable side-effects such as sedation, or a very dry mouth. In the event of this, discuss it with your doctor.

GWENDOLINE: Are there a lot of side-effects?

MARGARET: Like most other medications in use in other systems of the body, people may experience some side-effects. Often people are unreasonably anxious about taking what they see as 'mind-altering drugs' and this anxiety may exaggerate minor side-effects. It's worth remembering that some common remedies for head colds can make you feel sedated, and others can make you feel 'buzzy' or hyped up.

Your doctor should always tell you what side-effects are possible and what to do about them. Most side-effects are apparent in the early days of treatment and wear off as your body becomes accustomed to the medication.

Make sure the doctor is informed about any side-effects or other concerns the person has, encourage your loved one to do this directly or attend an appointment with them. Side-effects need to be acknowledged and can be managed, or medications can be changed.

GWENDOLINE: What should people look for in terms of how things change. Does your personality change?

MARGARET: The change is nearly always gradual and it may be a few weeks before people realise that they have recovered their zest for life. With any accompanying return of energy and motivation, it is often other people who start to notice some improvement. There are actual visible signs: the degree of animation in the facial expression, the tone of voice, the spontaneity of speech and actions. It's not a matter of the entire personality changing; people return to their normal degree of well-being.

GWENDOLINE: What other things do you suggest for people, Margaret, or is it as simple as just keeping on taking your medication?

MARGARET: The medication works to correct the imbalances, as we have discussed. But that's only part of the solution. Just as you would with a stomach ulcer or with asthma, you teach people how to manage their health in the future.

The other consideration is that when people are very depressed, there is only so much that they can take in at any one time. For that reason it is very helpful to have the nearest and dearest with them, so that you can get the message through on certain things.

I introduce the fact that the pills are one thing, but there are other things to do with the way you think and behave, the way you manage your stress, lifestyle, diet, etc. I try to get people to look at how they cope with problems, or get them to identify problem area. Often they are seeing a psychologist or therapist for that kind of support.

GWENDOLINE: Exactly, and it is these complementary treatments that we will be examining in the next few chapters. However, before we leave the biological treatments, I would like to briefly discuss ECT. I emphasise briefly, as Margaret and I both believe it is best discussed with the psychiatrist in person, given that it is such a daunting prospect for people.

ELECTROCONVULSIVE THERAPY (ECT)

For severely ill patients who have not responded to medication, ECT is considered to be a highly effective treatment. However, because of the misuse and overuse of ECT, it was a treatment that not only fell out of favour, but was actively lobbied against. There was concern about side-effects, in particular memory loss or brain damage. People were outraged at the thought that ECT was used a a punishment to control 'unpopular' behaviour as portrayed in *One Flew Over the Cuckoo's Nest.* There were also procedural concerns regarding the administration of ECT without anaesthetic.

What people are often not aware of are the improvements in the technique and that it is considered a very essential treatment option for patients at risk of suicide, or for the truly melancholic depressive who has stopped wanting to eat or drink and those that have not responded to medication. Another criticism has always been that it is not known exactly how the procedure works. However, this can also be said for certain heart disease medications or for phenytoin (Dilantin), which is used for seizure disorders.

ECT consists of a split-second shock of between 75 and 150 volts, a small and very safe current. This is done in an attempt to induce a seizure, and it is the seizure that is thought to be responsible for the cure.

Contemporary procedures involve the use of a general anaesthetic and a short-acting muscle relaxant, ensuring that the individual does not feel anything, and that the body does not convulse. Upon awakening there is some degree of confusion, and the person will tend to feel tired and somewhat fuzzy for the rest of the day. Following the completion of a course of treatments, which is usually between six and twelve, some people may report memory loss of events prior to the treatment. A colleague of mine describes these as more like 'holes' in your memory than large periods of time completely lost. While there may be patchy loss of previous memories, such as telephone numbers, after a few weeks, there is no continued impairment in the ability to memorise or learn new things.

The actual extent of memory impairment is almost impossible to measure accurately, as the memory loss could just as well be symptomatic of the depression, which also impairs memory.

This brief synopsis provides you with some of the technicalities, but what you must not hesitate to do is ask as many questions of your psychiatrist as you need to, to feel comfortable with the decision. If you don't feel that the psychiatrist is being sensitive to your needs and there is no rapport, change doctors. As a psychologist, I can't tell you much more about all the workings of the brain and what happens with ECT. As a person who has suffered the agonies of depression, I can tell you that if I had not responded to medication, I'd rather be hooked up to the national grid than live like that.

CHAPTER 4

Whose Couch is it Anyway!

WHAT we have established so far is that psychiatrists are medical experts who treat psychiatric illness with biologically based interventions. What I failed to mention, however, is that psychiatrists can be psychoanalysts and/or psychotherapists at the same time and offer some form of psychological support or counselling. Sigmund Freud, the father of psychoanalysis, was a psychiatrist, but you don't have to be one to be a psychoanalyst. In fact, you could be a psychologist or a psychotherapist who has trained in psychoanalysis. Essentially therapists, counsellors and psychologists do not practise medicine and are unable to prescribe medications.

So although your image of visiting the 'shrink', lying on the couch and being analysed, isn't completely wrong, your analyst may not be a psychiatrist and your psychiatrist may not have a couch. So, if you're all clear on that, we can move on!

This is undoubtedly one of the most confusing areas for people seeking help, especially with depression. Let's take a look at a very possible scenario: Your father was pushed into a situation of early redundancy. He's worked hard all his life and has never been very good at just relaxing. Over the months since his retirement, he has become increasingly withdrawn, has lost interest in all activities, and doesn't even enjoy a round of golf. He's become irritable and is driving your mother crazy. She's also becoming very anxious, as your grandmother committed suicide. You discuss it as a family and decide he needs help. Do you:

1. **Take turns, as a family, taking him out, making him play golf.**
2. **Go to a psychologist for retirement counselling.**
3. **Knowing that his mother took her life, find out if there is something in his childhood that he has never talked about. Should he be dealing with that?**
4. **Recognising symptoms of depression, go straight to your GP.**
5. **Take him straight to a psychiatric clinic.**

The following is ideally how things should take shape: Knowing that his mother committed suicide alerts us to the fact that there may be a genetic predisposition for depressive illness. Hence, the symptoms should be responded to immediately. Being of the 'old school', he will undoubtedly resist any interference and would be mortified at the suggestion of a psychiatrist. Your GP is the easiest option. Your doctor will either be able to prescribe and persuade him to take an antidepressant medication, or refer him to a psychiatrist. During this appointment, your GP would be the best person to suggest that he also attend some form of retirement counselling, as there are obviously social factors contributing to the onset of his depression. As he begins to feel better, encourage him to engage in outdoor activities, but don't force the issue.

The decisions that had to be made in this situation are primarily based around the choice between psychologically and biologically based treatments of depression, and how such choices should be prioritised You will undoubtedly find parallels with your own situation, which boil down to the same fundamental question: "Does the person just need to talk about it, or are drugs required?"

The likelihood is that your loved one is going to resist taking medication, but may agree to talk to somebody. This is something to be encouraged, as often an objective outsider can advise on the best course of treatment, avoiding arguments and conflict at home. A visit to your GP is often a good place to start, so that you can be pointed in the direction of a psychotherapist or psychiatrist, based on your doctor's medical opinion and knowledge of the family situation. However, it is still important that you have an understanding of the fundamental differences in the types of therapies available, so that the choice of therapist is an informed one. In her current state, your loved one is vulnerable and, because of her sense of desperation, can become gullible. The more knowledge you have, the more equipped you are to gauge improvement or deterioration in your loved one's mental state.

Psychodynamic Psychotherapy

A number of therapies fall within this category, the most well known being 'Freudian psychoanalysis'. This approach is based on the indeterminable search for the roots of the depression. The emphasis on 'indeterminable' relates to the duration of the therapy as well as the cost. Psychoanalysts are renowned for saying very little, but nodding their heads wisely a great deal. Their interest lies in the subconscious processes, they talk about transference and repression, and are intrigued with dreams and childhood memories. The philosophy is based on the belief that the current symptoms are a result of emotional damage incurred in the early stages of development, and it is the resolution of these unresolved childhood conflicts that lead to a cure.

Partially as a result of the aforementioned characteristics, psychoanalysis *per se* has fallen out of favour as a treatment of choice, even in America. It is not out of the realm of possibility for someone like Woody Allen to be in analysis for years and never address the current issues in his life. Other psychodynamic therapists have rejected the Freudian theory, have become more active in their approach, take a shorter time and cost less, but still rely on the basic principles.

The danger with this form of therapy for depressed people is that the rehashing of past unhappiness and trauma can overwhelm them, increasing the levels of their despair, taking them further into the black hole at a time when they are without the psychological resources to climb back out. As you've no doubt concluded by now, the effectiveness of this form of therapy in treating depression is questionable. Neither is there convincing research-based evidence to suggest otherwise.

Interpersonal Psychotherapy

This therapy places emphasis on the importance of social relations – how the individual copes with the everyday workings of getting on with other people. Far from concentrating on the past, the focus is on current interpersonal relationships and the provision of strategies and skills to improve this aspect of the person's life. Interpersonal therapy acknowledges that although depression is an illness, the causes can be environmental as well as biological, and that interpersonal relationship problems can be considered a significant contributing factor. Attention is paid to four main areas:

Abnormal grief reactions – has the individual become stuck, unable to move on from the sense of loss?

Conflicts – disruption within significant relationships.

Role transitions – dealing with retirement, divorce, leaving home, etc.

Social deficits – recurring problems with relationships, poor communication skills.

Interpersonal therapy is a brief intervention (12-16 weeks). It was originally designed as a therapy for people with depression of a mild to moderate severity. Because the aims are very concise, its effectiveness has been able to be measured, and it has been shown to contribute to the treatment of depression, particularly in conjunction with medication.

Cognitive Behaviour Therapy

Cognitive behaviour therapy (CBT) combines two very effective kinds of psychotherapy – cognitive therapy and behaviour therapy. The most widely used and systematically tested short-term therapy for depression, CBT is certainly recognised to be one of the most effective psychologically-based therapies in the treatment of depressed mood. Research also shows a good complementary relationship between CBT and the use of anti-depressant medication.

In this instance, the focus is on how the person thinks, working on the basic premise that negative, pessimistic thinking will perpetuate the depressed mood and accompanying behavioural patterns. It is a time limited and very structured approach. The relationship between the therapist and the patient is very collaborative and can resemble an educational partnership. With the emphasis on the sharing of information, under the guidance of an expert, helping to set treatment goals and objectives.

Depression knocks confidence and self-esteem, people think irrationally, and their ruminative thoughts are more often than not based on feelings of worthlessness and what a burden they are to everybody around them. Suicidal thoughts are very much centred around the belief of *"You would be better off without me."* The cognitive therapist encourages these people to work on refuting their irrational thoughts, drawing attention to more rational and optimistic ways of thinking and processing experiences. It is not however 'positive thinking – affirmation based' therapy. It is essentially challenging the self-critical and self-derogatory thinking, and replacing them with more rational and helpful alternatives, and at the same time acknowledging progress and change.

There can, however, be a Catch-22 situation that comes into play here. Is the person thinking negatively because he or she is depressed, or has thinking negatively caused the depression? It can sometimes be the case that as the depression is being treated medically (via medication) such thoughts are no longer present. Suicidal thoughts tend to be the most likely to disappear, however patterns of thinking that leave a person vulnerable to stress are frequently habitual and learned from childhood. Here again CBT provides techniques to help recognise these unhelpful ways of thinking and manage stress/distress in an ongoing and preventative manner. In fact you could probably have a look at a few of the techniques to manage your own stress levels at this time.

Supportive Counselling

I have chosen the word 'counselling' rather than 'therapy' in this instance, as the therapeutic relationship is primarily one of listening, offering reassurance where appropriate, educating around the experiences involved with depression, and providing a safe and comfortable environment in which to talk about how the person feels.

Supportive counselling has been seen as an option for those individuals who, as a result of the chronicity of their illness, are not expected to make fundamental changes. However, this type of support can also offer very real relief to those individuals waiting for the therapeutic benefits of their antidepressants to take effect.

Attending support groups, talking to perhaps a nurse or social worker, telephone counselling services, support through your church, all come under this general category. Being able to talk to somebody objective with a listening ear certainly can't do any harm.

Some of the Alternatives

There are numerous other forms of therapy that do not always get a mention in the more mainstream categories: primal scream therapy, rebirthing, Gestalt, regressive hypnotherapy, just to mention a few. These approaches are very self-focused, emphasising the need for emotional expression and catharsis. Again, there is no real evidence of their effectiveness and, as I mentioned earlier, I recommend caution with any technique that places emphasis on this degree of emotional expression at such a vulnerable time.

What I Did

Experiencing psychiatric illness has been one of the most profound learning curves of my life. As a psychologist, I had been trained to focus on the psychological and social causes of depression and, in response, look for psychologically based treatment strategies. On reflection, I don't think I ever placed much credence on medically based interventions. I actually remember thinking, "What's a pill going to do?" So, of course, when I started to become increasingly unwell, I got one hell of a shock!

Beside my bed was a stack of all the self-help books I had collected over the years. I would wake up each morning and flick through the pages, desperately trying to find something – a technique, an affirmation – anything to make me feel better. What happened was the opposite to what I had expected. My hands would start to tremble and I would end up being sick. Not being able to apply all these techniques to myself was making me feel like such a failure. How could I, as a *psychologist*, not be able to do these things and make them work?

Margaret, meanwhile, had asked me to consider antidepressants. However, I decided to go to a psychotherapist, as I was convinced that it was just a matter of 'getting my head back together'. I was also at this time still reeling from the profound spiritual content of my psychosis and felt that I needed to see somebody to help me sort through my experiences. I had been seeing Ellen for two weeks and, although I found our sessions helpful, I wasn't getting better.

Margaret insisted that I go on medication. I continued to go to therapy, initially twice a week, because I was getting something out of it, but the problem was that none of the positive feelings and perspectives I walked out with would stay with me any longer than an hour. However, at least I had relief from the torture of depression for that one hour, and that hour enabled me, on a good day anyway, to see that I could maybe have two of those hours in one day. With Ellen's help I was rediscovering hope. Ellen could not offer me a cure for the depression, but what she did offer was ways of dealing with my despair.

When the medication had taken effect, I discontinued my sessions. I was well on the way to recovery, I could feel myself returning. I am pleased that I sought out psychological help, as it did assist in getting me through some very difficult times. As with all depressed people, and your loved one is no different, I felt like such a burden to my nearest and dearest that there was something wonderful about being able to talk about how bad I was feeling and not feel guilty, because it was a professional arrangement.

Consequently, I approached Ellen and asked her to contribute to this chapter. She agreed that there was a real need not only to educate about what to expect from psychological treatments, but to 'demystify' the profession. With the range of therapies available and the jargon attached to them, it's not surprising that people get confused. It is this element of not knowing what to expect that places the person with the depression and the family into a powerless and vulnerable position. If your loved one is getting worse how do you know whether it is because he has a bad therapist? He may have been told that if he gets worse it's because he needs *more* therapy. The following are a few pointers that Ellen and myself came up with to help you make an evaluation of the therapist and/or the intervention.

THINGS TO LOOK OUT FOR

1

The treatment of depression needs to be collaborative – both biological and psychological components need to be addressed. Beware of therapists who will not work in conjunction with your loved one's doctor and/or psychiatrist – they are more interested in a power struggle over naming the problem than attending to what's best for their client.

2

Not all therapies are suited to all people. Sometimes individuals can start to feel that if they are not moving ahead in the recommended time frame they must be 'failing'. Encourage them to talk about how they feel the therapy is going. If they are doubtful and confused, ask if you can speak with the therapist,

3

Labelling someone's behaviour can also be destructive, for example, "You're depressed because you're a co-dependant". It is better that the therapist provides an opportunity to look at what the depression has meant in people's lives, how they understand it, how it affects their relationships with those around them, perhaps what lifestyle changes need to occur.

4

Don't be afraid to question therapists' qualifications and background. Ask what their qualifications are, perhaps contact someone else who has been to them, check out their reputations. Abuse does occur in professional relationships, particularly with the levels of vulnerability involved with being depressed. This degree of assertion may be too difficult for the depressed person, so this could be something that you follow through.

5

Scrutinise the effect of the therapy on your loved one. If you feel that she is getting worse, or if she is describing situations whereby she is feeling discounted, it could well be because of the therapist rather than the illness. The influence of an ineffectual or even corrupt therapist is very damaging, and the process is at times very insidious. If you feel that the therapist is at fault, you will need to extricate your loved one, because people who are depressed often feel they have lost their powers of discrimination and tend to blame it on themselves.

6

If your loved one is having difficulty remembering what happens each time, suggest taping the sessions, which will provide you with a means of checking things out. If you do not feel qualified enough to judge, network through your friends, and perhaps seek a second opinion.

In summary

There is more and more evidence to show that for clinically depressed people, anti-depressants in conjunction with cognitive therapy, followed by interpersonal therapy provide the most effective approach. Anti-depressants can work on their own, however when it is time to remove the medication the individual has not learned any stress management or coping skills to prevent possible relapse.

Supportive counselling is not scientifically attributed with any real therapeutic benefits in the treatment of depression but sometimes what's needed is just to be listened to.

It is my experience that the most effective treatment for depression is a combination of a psychologically based therapy and anti-depressants. To reiterate a point I have made previously, depression changes so many different facets of a person's life. Relationships are affected, as is self-esteem and confidence, and productive input in those specific areas can only enhance things in the long run.

As you will have gathered, there are many different types of psychologically based treatments, some more effective than others. One of the most important ingredients in their effectiveness is the skill of the therapist, not only in terms of technical skills, but also the ability to establish a sense of rapport with the client and the family. It is vital that you have confidence in the clinical aptitude and professionalism of the therapist. If you don't, find another one. You wouldn't buy a piece of clothing that didn't fit – why pay for a therapist who doesn't fit your requirements

CHAPTER 5

Pine, Honeysuckle & Water Violets

AS THE Flower Children of the seventies welcomed the dawning of the Age of Aquarius amidst clouds of marijuana smoke and LSD, behind the haze and endless pop tunes about San Francisco, the Rolling Stones acknowledged the dawning of the Age of Anxiety in the song 'Mother's Little Helper'.

Tranquillisers infiltrated our society under the guise of a harmless pharmacological panacea. They were reported as side-effect free and non-addictive. Worldwide, millions of people were prescribed these contemporary cure-alls. Problems started to occur, however, when people thought it was time to stop taking them. It was then that practitioners and scientists alike realised the enormity of this 'medical blunder'. What became very clear was that the pain and anxiety experienced as a result of the drug withdrawal were often far worse than the original symptoms of anxiety the drugs were designed to treat.

Emptying the Pill Bottles

As the multitudes of innocent victims throughout the world became increasingly aware of what had occurred, there was, of course, a huge public outcry. People raged against the medical profession and the drug companies that had made billions of dollars out of what had become a contemporary epidemic of human suffering. A manifestation of this rage was the denouncement of orthodox medicine.

When one reflects on those 'Halcyon Years', it is not surprising that in this the 'New Age' there is strong movement to ostracise orthodox medicine. Still reeling from the holocaust of benzodiazepine addiction, people would try anything before they would consider the use of medications for the treatment of mental ill-health.

Doctors were seen as drug-company whores, ready to prescribe the latest medication for a set of new golf clubs or a week in Club Med. These sentiments are, of course, perfectly understandable. However, I believe very strongly that the time has come to redress the balance.

Take a moment to think about your family doctor. Could you honestly say that you perceive him or her as a heartless drug pusher? That rather than being interested in helping patients, is keen to have them addicted to prescription drugs to make a quick buck on repeat prescribing. I'm not condoning the over-prescribing and mis-prescribing of anti-anxiety medications, but what I am suggesting is that it was not a matter of intentional malpractice. People continued to take them because they worked – they relieved anxiety. The problem was that they were highly addictive.

We now live in an age where depression has taken over from anxiety as the most common of all psychiatric disorders. However, in direct response to the huge medical and pharmacological blunder of the past 30 years, medical treatments are often considered to be one of the last options rather than the first.

Holistic Medicine

Although heralded as the treatment approach of choice in the nineties, it is my observation that this term is misunderstood by both the public and certain factions within the health professions. The word 'holistic' refers to the philosophy that 'the whole is greater than the sum of its parts', that is, all aspects of an individual – psychological, spiritual, emotional, cultural *and* physical – need to be addressed and taken into consideration.

A holistic approach, by definition, must acknowledge the contribution of medicine. The danger of certain schools of thought in the

'New Age' is their nihilistic view of medical practice, a scepticism that rejects orthodox medicine and, in doing so, interferes with the treatment of depression. I become very concerned when I talk with people who tell stories of their naturopath telling them to stop taking all their prescribed psychiatric medication, and take only the homeopathic or herbal remedies.

When someone is depressed, they don't eat or sleep properly, they become physically run down. Starved of adequate nutrients, the body accompanies the mind further into the depths of the depression. Through attending to these deficits, natural therapies are able to contribute to the overall treatment of the depression. It is this concept of contributing to 'wellness' that is truly holistic medical practice.

One could go on endlessly about all the academic, philosophical and ethical debates on New Age alternative healing versus traditional medicine, homeopathy versus drug therapy. But at the end of the day, when you're suffering you'll look anywhere and everywhere, and that's exactly what happens. People in pain search for relief, as I did, which led me to the waiting room of Karen, a Registered Naturopath and Remedial Body Therapist.

A Natural Approach

A couple of girlfriends had been telling me that when they get stressed they go for a massage, which really helps them get through difficult times. Eager to find the answer to what was wrong with me, this seemed like a very viable explanation. I was stressed. Simple as that. I, of course, wanted the first possible appointment Karen had available, because I knew that body massage was the answer.

I didn't inform Karen that I was depressed, mainly because I didn't know. I merely stated that I had been stressed lately and she came recommended. With a knot in my stomach the size of a football, I sat looking aimlessly around the room whilst Karen arranged several boxes of Bach flower potions on her desk. I was then asked to rest my hand on each box, while Karen dangled a pendulum over my hand to determine which collection of remedies I was 'responding' to.

After I had been taken through this procedure with all the different boxes, it was time for the massage. The towels were so wonderful and warm, and I remember Karen's hands moving assertively over my body, attempting to shift the tension from my muscles. Whilst I was getting dressed after the massage, feeling a little better, Karen left the room to mix up my homeobotanical remedy.

The magic potion was: S, E Pine Honeysuckle Water Violet. "Take 3 drops 3 times daily" it said on the bottle. Karen explained to me what everything was for and I immediately forgot everything she said. It didn't matter to me what it was, I just wanted it to work. I would have eaten a bunch of water violets, or for that matter made a decent dent in a pine tree if I'd thought it was going to make any difference. Karen recommended that I make another appointment. I didn't, because as I moved towards the door of her office, I could feel all the pains of the anxiety and depression returning, and I began to dry retch as I turned the key in my car door. The '3 drops 3 times a day' didn't work, the multi-vitamins got stuck in my throat, and the spirulina drinks made me heave.

As I have mentioned previously, your loved one, just as I was, is likely to be looking for alternatives to medication, and although natural remedies may not be harmful, reliance on them as the sole means of treatment can delay seeking other help. You also need to be very wary of natural therapists who discount other proven interventions.

Nature's Alternatives

Based on my own experiences, I believe that natural therapies should enhance and work alongside conventional treatments. Here's a review of a few of them and some thoughts from a naturopath about the part natural therapies can play in the treatment of depressive illness. I have not attempted to provide detailed information on all the various types of natural therapies. I have concentrated on naturopaths as the 'general practitioners' of natural healing. The first step in any treatment regimen is an accurate diagnosis, and I asked Karen if she felt that training in naturopathy enabled her to diagnose depression.

KAREN: Well, probably not. I could tell if there was something wrong after maybe a couple of sessions, and suggest that the person go to the doctor, but the symptoms of depression? I'm not sure enough of them to say that's exactly what a person would be suffering from. I have helped a lot of people who describe what they are feeling as depression. But I think a lot of people use that word even when they are just feeling a bit down. They are the easy ones to help because I can relieve the stress in their bodies partly through massage, getting them to look at what they eat, looking at allergies, suggesting whole foods instead of refined foods, checking on blood sugar counts, and I also work with Bach flowers.

GWENDOLINE: Having gone through the Bach flower and pendulum experience I was interested to know the philosophy behind this practice, which I must admit seemed more like magic than anything else.

KAREN: You interpret the pendulum by which way it swings. It turns around if it's a 'yes' and just keeps going back and forward if it's a 'no', and that indicates which combination of Bach flowers to use in the homeobotanical remedy. I don't know how that works – it's a real mystery to me. I just know that it does work, so there *is* a little bit of magic in there, which has never done anyone any harm. I know that for sure and I know that it has done a lot of good.

Bach flower remedies work on Dr Bach's idea that every emotion has a positive and negative, and that you might as well be living with the positive side of that emotion as the negative side. They don't change people's emotions, because that isn't something we would want to do, because our emotions are valid, so this just turns the emotion around to its positive side. I have found this technique to be useful for people who are feeling a bit down, but not for those suffering from severe depression.

All of these things can help minimise stress. If people don't seem to be responding, referring them to their doctor would be the next step. I have found that doctors are good at referring people to specialist services if that's required. I'm always careful about which doctor I refer people to, because I would hate it if they went to one who would just put them on Valium or something similar, but that doesn't happen so much any more.

GWENDOLINE: I become very concerned, as a clinician, when people are required to make a choice between their doctor and their natural therapist. Is this part of the naturopathic philosophy?

KAREN: No, because depression is a chemical imbalance in your body. Diet can help that, but I think by the time people are really depressed they need some strong medicine to turn them around. And then, after they've done that, I'm really happy to help them stay well. I would prefer that to be my role.

I tend to get a little bit nervous when I have clients who don't want to take any drugs and will only consider natural methods. I tell them that I would prefer them to seek medical advice and that maybe some of the drugs aren't so bad these days. I would like to know more about this area, as I know the drugs are not so addictive now, but I need to know more to tell my clients. I'm always happier if people will see other professionals as well as me.

Other people I see may be on antidepressants, and know they need them at the time, but are really happy to be able to add something natural as well, and with Bach flowers I know that they're safe and won't stop the antidepressants working.

I won't discard all forms of orthodox medicine – I think that can be quite dangerous. People will go to all sorts of lengths to try natural remedies, but I have never had good enough results with severe depression. There is a lot of advice in the literature about vitamins, minerals, protein, natural ways of enhancing serotonin, but I am against giving people false hope.

GWENDOLINE: Do you think doctors are as tolerant and understanding of the potential contribution of natural alternatives?

KAREN: One of the things that makes me really mad about some doctors is that they say to people, "There's nothing that can be done for you." It is at times like this that people will come to me in desperation, and there is always something that can be done. If not magical cures, relief of symptoms. I think we need to get rid of the notion that one group of health professionals can cure everything.

GWENDOLINE: This is really the key to what we have discussed. It is again the concept of alternative treatments working in partnership. In researching this book I did speak with a homeopath who reported great success working with suicidally depressed patients, describing a cure after one treatment. However, such anecdotal examples have not been substantiated by medical research.

St. John's Wort

During the late 1990's media attention and the resulting public interest saw St. John's Wort (SJW) elevated to 'herbal superstar status'. In 1998 alone, world consumption of SJW was 7000 tonnes; this is of course is a reflection of all of the issues that have been raised earlier on in this chapter. However, despite the presence of trends in alternative medicine, the main questions to be posed remain the same:

Are the extracts safe?
Does SJW reduce depressive feelings? and
Should we recommend it's use?

Researchers do indicate that there is scope for alternative anti-depressants, more so for the mild types of depression, if they can be shown to be safe and effective. From reviewing the literature here are my thoughts for consideration:

- Available evidence and research for SJW is insufficient at this stage, with some of the research being influenced by the pharmaceutical companies and, from the other side of the fence research being conducted that biases against orthodox medicines. Further research needs to be conducted.

- There needs to be a far better quality control of the herbal preparations, they currently are subject to fewer checks than registered drugs.

- The combinations of SJW with other medications also need to be closely monitored, asking the question should non-medical prescribing occur?

- Given that one of the aims of the treatment of depression is the prevention of suicide, the use of treatment not fully investigated could increase the risk and delay the introduction of proven interventions. Also in a climate where SJW does not require a medical prescription or supervision, the identification of suicidal risk is not possible. This has real implications particularly in the treatment of children and young adults, as well as with the medical conditions that mimic depression such as hypothyroidism.

On the other hand such remedies available over-the-counter could be useful for people with what we call 'sub-clinical' (very mild) depression that are unlikely to be treated otherwise. I do feel that natural therapies can attend to the imbalances that occur as a result of the anxiety and inadequate dietary habits of the depressed person, and natural remedies are something that you may wish to consider. You are not depressed, but you are stressed and distressed by this experience. Herbal remedies such as chamomile are used for nerves and agitated stomachs, and it's a lot better than grabbing a bottle of Valium. Likewise, if you're having trouble sleeping, valerian is recognised as a natural antidote for stress, and helps insomnia. Don't forget to look after yourself!

POINTS TO TAKE FROM THIS CHAPTER

1

People often use the word 'depression' to describe feeling a bit down or a bit stressed. This is not the same as clinical depression. Natural therapies may be helpful in the relief of stress-related symptoms, but if these symptoms persist, it's time to see a doctor.

2

If your loved one is currently on prescription medication, this should not be stopped without discussing it with your doctor. Natural therapists are not specialists in the treatment of depression and are not trained in the intricacies of psychiatric medications.

3

Beware of natural therapists who demand the cessation of all prescription medications prior to beginning their treatment intervention. A skilled and professional therapist will be willing to work alongside other health professionals

4

Natural remedies for stress are worth considering for yourself.

CHAPTER 6

… *& the Kneebone's Connected to the Thighbone*

REMEMBER that little ditty, "Dem bones, dem bones, dem dry bones…". What I want to know is, does anybody remember if there was a bit that said:

> "…*And the head bone's connected to the neck bone,*
> *And the neck bone's connected to the torso bone.*
> *And if that's the way it is, that must mean that*
> *The mind's connected to the 'body' bone…*
> *mmm, …oh yeah.*"

The point that I raise is how quickly we forget that the mind and the body work together. You have undoubtedly been so preoccupied with caring for your loved one that you don't even realise how much stress you are under. It may sound like a complete contradiction in terms, but the reality is that looking after someone with a depressive illness over a long period of time becomes a burden.

You may be thinking, "How can she suggest that caring for someone I love is a burden – the audacity!" It's got nothing to do with how much you love them – it's exhausting. In the early stages of care you may even think it sacrilegious to feel irritated and frustrated with the lack of change and the absence of any improvement. What you have to realise is that this isn't the 'flu – it is not an illness that is going to go away over-night, or after a ten-day course of medication.

The convalescence period takes months.

If your loved one is openly expressing suicidal thoughts, or has at times been actively suicidal, you are going to worry. You love them and you don't want to leave them in case anything happens. When you're with them you're worrying, and when you're away from them you will be doing exactly the same thing. Don't think for one moment that these levels of stress are not going to take their toll.

In the previous chapter I suggested that you may wish to look at a few natural remedies. Now we're going to concentrate on **you** looking after **your** physical and emotional well-being. Your emotions will also be taking a hammering during this time. Your loved one's lack of response to all that you have been doing can be very hurtful. The more time you dedicate to your loved one, the more you start to get behind at work – you have less time for leisure, the family starts to suffer, your own quality of life starts to erode. You are allowed to have emotions, you are allowed to feel something about all this.

Having been brought up in a society that has denied the importance of emotional expression and places 'stiff upper lips' on a pedestal, it's not surprising that you may feel reluctant to share your feelings with others. However, the reality is that if you don't acknowledge these things, you put yourself at risk. The following is an introduction to some of the research findings in this area. I often find that providing people with scientific explanations of how they are feeling gives them permission to do something tangible about resolving them.

Researchers Petrie, Booth and Davison found strong evidence to suggest that if an individual is for some reason prevented from discussing stressful events in life, it may cause the immune system to dysfunction, increasing the likelihood of illness.

So to relate this to your situation, during the weeks and months since your loved one became unwell, there will have been times when you have felt frustrated and angry with her. You may, at times, have felt a little resentful that you can't get on with your own life. You tell yourself that it is terrible to even think such things, and immediately feel guilty. These feelings of guilt and your fear of making things worse can actively inhibit you from expressing yourself and your needs.

J.W. Pennebaker, a well-known researcher in the area of 'inhibition', went so far as to state: "...actively holding back or inhibiting our thoughts and feelings can be hard work. Over time, the work of inhibition gradually undermines the body's defences. Like other stressors, inhibition can affect immune function, the action of the heart and vascular systems, and even the biochemical workings of the brain and nervous systems. In short, excessive holding back of thoughts, feelings and behaviours can place people at risk for both major and minor diseases."

So, there you have it, with the science to prove it. You need to take care of yourself emotionally, particularly at this time. You'll be of no use to anyone if you burn out, and remember, your mind is connected to your body just like everybody else. The following list contains a list of the signs of stress you need to look out for.

As you will probably notice a number of these symptoms are similar to those listed for depressive illness. It is not an uncommon experience for people living with a depressed person for any length of time to end up feeling depressed themselves.

POSSIBLE REACTIONS TO STRESS

1

Irritability, feeling very short-tempered with the family or people at work.

2

Becoming obsessional about little things. Being plagued by unwanted thoughts.

3

Muscular tension, back aches, neck aches, stomach cramps.

4

Tension headaches.

5

Indigestion.

6

Constipation or diarrhoea.

7

Lack of interest in food or excessive overeating.

8

Constantly feeling tired.

9

Disturbed sleeping patterns.

What You Can Do to Help Yourself?

In researching advice in this area I have focused on very practical and non-demanding suggestions. There is nothing worse than a self-help guide that you need professional advice to interpret. Also, at this time, don't put pressure on yourself to absorb a lot of new and complicated information. You need to keep things simple to ease the pressure.

The following activities and suggestions may also be of benefit to your loved one. However, they may not feel *able* to participate. It is not that they just don't want to. If this is the case, don't worry, go out and do them for yourself. You can only encourage your loved one to get involved – pushing too hard is counter-productive.

TALK ABOUT HOW YOU FEEL

- Make phone calls to friends or family members – start 'sharing the load'.
- Don't be reluctant to involve the family or other friends – it makes it easier for everybody.
- Switch off the television for a while in the evening and talk to your partner/the family, or have a friend over.

- *Remember*, you're talking about how *you* feel, not what the depressed person is feeling. This is for your well-being.

PHYSICAL COPING SKILLS

1

Find a course that teaches relaxation techniques including breathing exercises, for example, yoga, Tai Chi, meditation.

DINAH: Make sure you are going to a reputable practitioner who teaches good physiological breathing. You need to concentrate on how to relax the upper chest, as that's where all the tension is.

There are numerous tapes available that teach relaxation techniques and I have also recommended books in the suggested reading list on page 155.

2

Learn to massage each other's necks – use touch rather than words to provide comfort. This can involve the entire family, as well as the family member who is depressed.

3

Organise time out of the house. You're not just taking a break, you are taking care of your own health. Needing time away doesn't mean you love the depressed person any less.

4

In a family situation or amongst friends, take turn about. When someone is depressed, it's important that there is human presence, but the whole family doesn't need to be there. It's a very easy thing to say, "Look, Mum, I'm going to be home tonight, why don't you go out".

5

Book yourself into the hot pools, or get a professional massage once a week. Just go off and relax, eat chocolate if you want to (not too much!). You're not just allowed to, you have to.

6

Look for something physical to do that requires no mental energy, for example, chopping wood, gardening, stroking your pet, or throwing stale bread at a few unsuspecting ducks.

7

Catch up with friends, or go to a movie to take your mind off things for a while. I'd recommend comedy over drama just at the moment.

8

And last, but by no means least, there is another phenomenon, highly acclaimed for its healing powers. Dinah recommends it as it's known "to collapse the chest, utilise the diaphragm and enhance better breathing" ... LAUGHTER.

WRITE ABOUT YOUR FEELINGS

- Don't worry about what you're writing, or how well you're doing – it's not a creative writing course. What's important is expressing how you're feeling.
- Don't use writing as a way of avoid talking through problems. It is most helpful as a way of exploring your thoughts and gaining a little perspective.
- You don't have to show your writing to anybody, but you may find it a useful way to break the ice and begin a communication with your loved one about how the depression is affecting you and/or the family.

The above suggestions concentrate on your thoughts and emotions and the importance of 'getting things off your chest'. By doing so you are taking care of yourself physically as well as mentally. The next set of coping skills focuses primarily on the physical. Dinah Bradley, a good friend and respiratory therapist, helped me put this list together, at the same time explaining why we need to pay attention to the strictly physical side of stress.

One of Dinah's first comments was how people have lost their 'body sense'. For instance, they may be unaware of muscle tensions and changes in breathing when anxious. Many people have lost the knack of how to switch off from their problems, and at the moment you are probably worrying every waking hour.

DINAH: We keep stress levels going when we're constantly thinking about a problem. Our heart rates go up, our elbows tighten, our hands get sweaty, and all of these things add to the discomfort.

When you are so attached to the one you love, his or her distress can almost become catching. You find yourself not taking breaks and getting away. You can also start to mirror your loved one's breathing patterns. Often, if you're sitting with someone who's gulping in breaths or breathing fast, you start breathing in the same way. Families, in fact very often breathe alike. This is particularly evident when dealing with hyperventilation.

Dinah's comment about the breathing patterns of families reminds us of just how connected families are, at the same time highlighting the need for support for the whole family, especially during times of crisis. It is too easy to be united around the illness, to reinforce each other's sense of despair, to let gloominess pervade. From the point of view of the depressed person, she only feels increasingly guilty about the effect she is having on you, but unfortunately there is nothing she can do right now. What you can do is to try and maintain some sense of normalcy. Remember when you used to go for long walks, breathing in the air and picking the occasional flower from other people's gardens? You can still do that, in fact, try this helpful little breathing exercise while you're at it!

Slow-Breathing Technique

Try doing this exercise at least four or five times a day – it doesn't take a lot of time or effort and will help with your tension.

Hold your breath and count to ten (don't make the mistake of taking a deep breath.)

When you get to ten, breathe out and try saying to yourself the word 'relax', in a calm and soothing manner.

Breathe in and out slowly in a six second cycle. Breathe in for three seconds and out for three seconds. This will produce a breathing rate of ten breaths per minute. Breathe in a smooth and light manner.

At the end of each minute (after ten breaths) hold your breath again for ten seconds and then continue breathing in the six-second cycle.

Continue breathing in this manner until the symptoms of tension and perhaps any over breathing have gone.

CHAPTER 7

The Forgotten Link

A wise man will hear, and will increase learning;
and a man of understanding shall attain unto wise counsels.
(Proverbs 1:5)

THE purpose of the first part of this book has been to provide you with information on what sort of help is available, as well as give you some understanding of the strengths and pitfalls of the various approaches. So far, the focus has been on health-based services: psychology, naturopathy, psychiatry, etc. What did occur to me, however, is that the missing and often 'forgotten link' when dealing with depressed people and their loved ones is their relationship with their church, their chosen spiritual beliefs and/or their spirituality as it relates to their culture.

Spirituality remains a very important dimension of people's lives, regardless of whether or not they practise orthodox religion. It is inherent, intrinsic, inseparable from who we are. Through our culture, our mythology and symbols, our memories and dreams, it is our ancestry.

I am not about to address the differences between the various religious denominations, nor is it possible in this context to specifically attend to the diversity of the multi-cultural society. I do believe, however, that it is important to acknowledge an individual's faith and one's concept of 'spirituality', and to incorporate this 'spiritual community' within the support system for the depressed person and the family. I use the term 'spiritual community' to embrace the more orthodox concept of the church community, and those communities more attached to the family's cultural origins of spirituality.

As a result of viewing depressive illness from a purely psychological and psychiatric perspective, health professionals have traditionally been very guilty of negating the importance to individuals of their spiritual beliefs and, by doing so, overlooking the valuable support and sense of belonging this community can offer. There are numerous reasons for this, some of which I shall touch on, but the most important point at this junction is that you feel you can assert your own and your loved one's needs in this area.

The other very pragmatic consideration is that, in rural communities in particular, intervention and support by way of psychiatrists and psychologists are not always readily available, and, hence, not always an immediate option. Regardless of where you live, it may be that the person you feel you can trust the most with your distress and concern is your minister or spiritual counsellor. Particularly if you had no real concept of depression as an illness requiring medical help, you would understandably turn to a relationship where you feel safe.

In the process of putting this book together, I spoke with a couple who had recently been through the tortures of post-natal depression. It was an enormous step for this woman to tell her husband that she felt like hurting their newborn baby. Where do you go with something like that? It doesn't sound like an illness, but it does sound frightening. They went to their minister and, in response to his advice, sought medical help.

As a clinician listening to this story, it emphasised two very significant points: first, what an important support the minister had provided for the family, and, secondly, how he had acted as a trustworthy referral source and advised them to seek specialised help. Once again, I was reminded of how elitist and disconnected the various health professions can become, and that if we are serious about the 'holistic' approach, practitioners need to communicate.

Healing comes from co-operation, not competition.

Wanting to examine these issues further, I spoke with Paul and William, two delightful clergymen. William had also trained as a psychotherapist. (Note, as I mentioned earlier, it has not been possible for me to incorporate all denominations. Hence in this discussion we speak very generally about spirituality and support from, in this instance, a church-based community. The concepts, however, can be applied globally.

The main purpose of this discussion is to help you determine both the contributions as well as the limitations of spiritual counsel and support when dealing with a loved one suffering from depressive illness.

GWENDOLINE: In your role as clergymen, you must work a lot with families coping with various types of psychiatric ill-health. What do you feel you can offer?

WILLIAM: Something I noticed when I ran a therapy centre attached to a church in London was that people found that the actual building was very symbolic – they found it very comforting and secure.

I have found that a lot of friends and relatives of people who are disturbed in different ways are supported by church communities, even if the person themselves does not actually use the church. counselling. In fact, I don't work as a Christian psychotherapist, and my psychotherapy is not Christian-based. If anyone says they need to see a Christian counsellor for psychological and psychiatric-based problems, I shudder.

GWENDOLINE: So in terms of working with a person with depression, how do you perceive your role?

PAUL: I think sometimes people assume that because you're a minister, or priest, or because you wear a dog collar, you're actually trained as a therapist. There are people in need coming in for counselling all the time, but just talking and listening to people isn't psychotherapy. Both William and myself are clear about separating spiritual guidance from counselling and psychotherapy.

I see a lot of people wanting to learn about themselves, *but there's often a blurring between when it is spiritual direction they require and when it is shifting into psychotherapy.* It is important to know when something is emerging that may require another form of help. I believe it's important, as a minister, to have in my tool kit a whole referral system and know when to use it. We seek to be professional in that area of our work, and consider ourselves accountable for what we do.

GWENDOLINE: On the subject of knowing when to refer people to a specialist, I think it is so important that all helping professionals are trained in how to recognise depressive illness. Would you agree?

PAUL: I think that is absolutely necessary. There should be opportunities to provide that sort of training for prospective clergy, and not just clergy, but licensed people in the church. One approach would be through Clinical Pastoral Education. I do believe as clergy we need to be more clear about the skills we do have, because too often the clergy are set up to be Jacks of all trades.

GWENDOLINE: So you feel quite comfortable working alongside a medical approach to depression?

WILLIAM: Certainly. In fact I have no hesitation in suggesting to my clients that they consider going to their doctor for antidepressants, although they tend to be resistant. I explain to them that they have got into a circle of depression, and they keep going around and around. The antidepressants actually enable that circle to be broken, and then you can work with them from other angles. Situations don't change for them, but their perceptions will and their ability to change things. It gives power back to people, whereas depression takes power away from them.

GWENDOLINE: I ask that question because I am aware that people with depression can appear within a spiritual framework to be undergoing a crisis of faith whereas in actuality it is the depression that has created the existential crisis.

WILLIAM: Certainly there is a nervousness among the clergy with regards psychiatry and drug therapy. Just as I know that among a lot of psychotherapists and psychiatrists there is a total dismissal of the spiritual professions. It is as if they are dismissed as being well-meaning amateurs with no status.

I've not had many psychologists and psychiatrists ring me up as part of the treatment of depression, whereas I always make contact with the doctor or health professional. I've found that being taken seriously by doctors, as part of the professional team, is very rare. Perhaps their experiences with the clergy have been useless, I don't know, I mean some psychiatrists and psychologists are useless.

PAUL: It's as if they ignore the fact that spirituality is an issue for people in their lives. There's a spiritual need, a deep primitive, human need for rites of passage and transition. Having these spiritual needs represented and heard by the doctors or psychiatrists hopefully challenges their assumptions and perceptions and, in doing so, brings in another dimension.

GWENDOLINE: That is such an important point, given that one of the environmental factors that can contribute to the onset of depression is unresolved grief, and that an important part of the psychological resolution of grief is through the ritual and symbology of rites of passage.

I'd like to emphasise at this point the difference between grief and depression. Depression can follow a significant loss, but grief is not depression. Hence the approach in terms of resolution is quite different. Grief can be resolved through psychological counselling and/or through spiritual counsel, whereas in the treatment of depression, spiritual guidance is only one component of the overall 'healing package'.

PAUL: That's so true. There is no quick fix. The danger with so many therapies is that they become elitist. It's not as simple as the acupuncturist who will take away your disease, the confessor who will take away your guilt, and the cure-all faith healer. We need to work together with the psycho-therapist, the reflexologist, the psychiatrist. Know what we can do, the skills we have and the skills of our colleagues.

GWENDOLINE: Another very sobering fact with depressive illness is that people do commit suicide. It is analogous to any chronic illness in that death is the final outcome.

Depression as an illness attacks what I describe as the psychological immune system. By that, I refer to the immunity we gain from hope and optimism. People don't become depressed because they question their faith – depression strips a person of both hope and faith. Certainly, it can be an important part of their recovery to address issues of a spiritual nature, but this process in itself will not cure a depressive illness.

A FEW PROVERBS OF MY OWN

1

As a family member or very dear friend, you may need to seek out your own spiritual guidance and support from the community.

2

A healthy, spiritually based community is able to create an ethos of appropriate support and care for people, regardless of whether or not they attend the group regularly.

3

Request that your spirituality/cultural beliefs be acknowledged when dealing with the various health professions.

4

You may choose to deal with your anguish through a spiritual outlet, seeking out the support of your church and the community. But hoping if only your loved one would regain her faith the depression would go away is not practical, as it is unlikely to happen.

5

Grief and depression are not the same. Because it is an illness, depression needs to be treated as such.

6

If your loved one is looking for a cure by means of faith healing, try to encourage her to read educational material, as a lot of important time can be wasted in this pursuit.

7

Scientific research has proven the healing power of prayer.* It has been found that in times of great loss, prayer acts in the same way as talking with friends – it is a form of disclosure or confiding.

8

Your spiritual counsellor or minister is not traditionally trained in psychotherapy or psychiatric diagnosis. However, they can be of great support at this time, and may also be able to guide you in the right direction if you don't know which way to turn.

* See Pennebaker, 1990.

CHAPTER 8

Cry Baby Cry

I DON'T know if the Beatles were making reference to post-natal depression when they wrote their song *Cry Baby Cry*, but you never know what goes on behind closed doors. Wishing your newborn baby was dead certainly isn't something you'd want to tell the world about. In fact, it is such a shameful and frightening experience for those women who experience such feelings that they don't want to tell anybody about it, which accounts for the small percentage who present for treatment versus the phenomenal number of women who suffer from it. It is estimated that more that half of all mothers can be affected by post-natal depression.

So why don't they go for treatment? A lot of the reasons we have discussed in previous chapters also apply in this instance: they are afraid of appearing 'mentally ill', incompetent of looking after their child, or of being locked in an institution. The other factor is that although they may know that something is wrong, they don't know what it is. They may at first think, "Oh, it's just 'Baby Blues', no big deal." Then as time progresses and they are feeling more distressed and estranged from the newborn baby, guilt, inadequacy and self-blame take hold. By this stage they hate themselves, they hate the baby and they're convinced that you and everybody else around them hates them as well. What they also know for sure is that they are hopeless mothers and should never have fallen pregnant. Why talk to a doctor about that?

You may know that something is very wrong, but because of your emotional involvement, may be unsure of what it is. The other confusing aspect is that not all women experience the same symptoms, and often it is quite some time after the birth of the baby that the symptoms occur.

Could it be One of These?

BABY BLUES

During the first week after delivery, up to 70 per cent of women suffer some of the symptoms of what is known as the 'Baby Blues'. The symptoms are as follows:

Physical

- Not sleeping well and feeling tired after sleeping.
- No energy.
- Food cravings or loss of appetite.

Psychological

- Feeling constantly anxious.
- Lacking in confidence and feeling "I'm not myself."
- Overwhelming feelings of sadness.
- Feeling confused and nervous.

Reactions

- Irritability with everyone.
- Feelings hurt easily and hence crying a lot
- Lack of feeling for the baby.

Although these symptoms may pass quickly, it is still a very distressing time for mothers. There is no one cause and neither are some women more likely to suffer than others. Research suggests a number of contributing factors: hormonal changes, physical and mental stresses of labour, and the level of technological intervention during birth.

Medical intervention is not required unless these symptoms last longer than two weeks. In this case, a more serious depression may have developed, which needs treatment. The best help you can offer is to listen to the mother's feelings and ease any pressure by helping in very practical ways.

POST-NATAL PSYCHOSIS

This is the most severe but, fortunately, the most rare form of maternal depression. Surveys indicate that in most cases symptoms begin within two weeks of birth. The symptoms are as follows:

Physical

- Refusal to eat.
- Inability to stop being busy.
- Frantic excessive energy.
- Loss of sexual interest.

Psychological

- Extreme confusion, feelings of guilt and remorse.
- Loss of memory.
- Becoming quite incoherent.
- Thoughts of suicide.
- Bizarre hallucinations, delusions (belief in things that aren't real).
- Thoughts of infanticide (killing the baby).

Reactions

- Suspiciousness.
- Preoccupation with trivial matters.
- Irrational statements and reactions.

Once again, the causes are not fully understood, but the following hypotheses have been put forward: a previous history of a similar disorder; close relatives with similar disorders; biochemical and/or psychological stress associated with childbirth.

Post-natal psychosis is a very serious condition and medication and psychiatric care are essential. Short-term hospitalisation may be required for the safety of both mother and child. It is an acute illness, not a chronic disease, with 95 per cent of sufferers recovering after treatment.

POST-NATAL DEPRESSION

What is often mystifying is that post-natal depression may not occur directly after birth and can appear gradually up to two years later. The severity of symptoms differs amongst women, as does the number of symptoms they may experience.

Physical

- Sleep disturbance, unable to get to sleep, waking early.
- Headaches.
- General pains and feelings of being unwell, for example, chest pains, heart palpitations.
- Hyperventilation, panic attacks.
- Loss of sexual interest.
- Marked change in appetite.

Psychological

- Despondency and despair.
- Feeling inadequate, unable to cope.
- A sense of hopelessness and powerlessness.
- Inability to concentrate, think clearly or remember.
- Thoughts of suicide, strange thoughts or fantasies.
- Lack of interest in activities once enjoyed.
- Excessive concern over baby's health.
- Feelings of shame, embarrassment or guilt.

Reactions

- Extreme or unusual behaviour.

- Anxiety along with new fears/phobias.
- Not wanting to go out or to be with people.
- Nightmares.
- Feelings of being out of control, of 'going crazy'.
- No feelings for the baby or anger towards the baby.
- Extreme guilt.

Contributing Factors

There are numerous contributing factors, from hormonal to social problems. The following are thought to increase the risk factor for women:

- Stressful or unplanned pregnancy.
- Difficult childbirth.
- Isolation, lack of family support.
- Career change from paid employment, with loss of identity, especially for women over 30.
- Recent death of a close friend or family member.
- Previous abortion, cot death, stillbirth.
- Unresolved issues from own childhood/poor relationship with own mother.
- Increased workload at home, especially with a 'difficult' baby.
- Juggling a career and a new baby.

As you can see, there are similarities amongst the three types of maternal depression I have outlined. The most important thing to realise is that it is an illness that can be treated, and endless suffering is unnecessary.

Both medication and psychologically based therapy can be useful. There are numerous resource books, services and support groups available.

Support groups can be particularly helpful in that they help take away some of the feelings of, "Oh God, I'm the only woman in the world who wasn't ever supposed to have children!" However, support groups are primarily set up for the mothers themselves, leaving friends and family none the wiser. Because identifying with the stories of others seems to help all those involved. I spoke to a woman who was prepared to share her experiences.

Wendy's Story

I think the hardest thing is recognising that it is an illness, that you can explain your behaviour in those terms. It was a really important realisation for my husband, because all he felt was my complete lack of interest, my hostility. I just wanted to sleep all day, not do anything. I had no energy or enthusiasm for anything and it was just rotten.

At first I would pass it off to the fact that I was just a little bit tired, as my daughter wasn't sleeping right through. My husband and I went on holiday, thinking that the rest would make a difference, but it didn't – I had a miserable time. Six months after the birth, my mood was still going down and down and down. Christmas arrived and we were having the family at home, but I didn't want to do anything, I just wanted them all to go away. I wasn't interested and just kept on making excuses for not doing things.

I tried to go back to work in January, and managed to work for one week, but then I started to wake up crying every day. Initially, I thought I was simply not coping with being a mother and that and I would just have to work through it. I tried to pull myself together but it just got worse and worse and worse.

I found that I had no interest in my other children – it wasn't just the baby. I couldn't be bothered with them. I would have been quite happy to have curled up, gone to sleep and not woken up. I remember driving over the bridge one day and planning my own funeral. I then started to feel that this wasn't me, this was not normal.

My husband was at breaking point and he asked if I thought we needed marriage guidance counselling. He felt that I was giving him nothing and I was so emotionally bereft that I felt I had nothing to give anybody. But I just kept trying to cope with work, my husband, the kids. It was ten months before I decided to see a psychiatrist and get some treatment.

It was my GP who suggested I do something. I was very resistant to thinking of it as a disease, even though I come from a medical background. When you think of depression you think everybody will suspect that you're a bit loopy, you're nutty and you're going to go to a mental hospital. I didn't want anybody to think that of me, because I was always seen as someone who copes and very much a 'doer'. So you worry about other people's perceptions and you don't want to admit the fact that you have an illness.

I talked it over with my husband, but the decision to get treatment needed to come from me. He couldn't see that I was depressed, even though his background is also medical. You just can't see it in your close relatives. My parents got angry with me because I never wanted to do anything. They had very little comprehension of what was going on.

Now that I'm well, I realise that the hardest thing to come to grips with is that you have an illness – that is treatable. After a couple of weeks on the tablets the difference was phenomenal! You think to yourself, "I've been going on like this for so long for nothing. I've actually almost tried to destroy my marriage and my family by keeping on going like this." I started to feel so much more together and my energy to do things came back.

GWENDOLINE: Wendy, when you look back, what did you want from your family? What did you want them to do for you?

WENDY: It was difficult because I didn't know what was going on myself. I'm used to being in charge and being the leader, so because I didn't exactly know what I wanted or needed, I didn't know how I wanted them to react. My husband tried all sorts of different ways. At times he was very cool and calm and just left me alone. I didn't want that. At other times, he tried to be quite supportive, be kind and nice, and I couldn't appreciate that – I never even used to say thank you. The easiest thing for him to do was to pack me in the car and take me to see a psychiatrist, but I didn't want that either at first.

My mother-in-law actually noticed that I hadn't been myself since the birth of our daughter. She commented, but not very directly. People don't like to say things to you directly, they just think you're feeling a bit down at the time and you'll come right and pick yourself up. My mother tends to see it that way, that you'll just straighten yourself up.

I think what family members have to understand is that it's a disease and it's going to take a lot of time to heal. It's the time factor that's really important. It's easy to forget quite quickly and a lot of people haven't got the patience and the time to understand what's going on. Because depression takes so long to treat – a three to six month minimum period – it's very hard for somebody to be patient and supportive for that length of time when you haven't got something that's obviously outwardly wrong.

One of the things that I do is to go on purpose into the bathroom in the mornings and take my antidepressant while my husband's watching. By doing that I feel that he knows I'm still not very well and not completely back to normal.

It can be very frustrating for the family. They may think that you're taking longer than you need to, and that maybe you're just being lazy. It's important that they know they are in for a long haul, and remember that you're not up to what you were able to do before you were sick. You can't get back into it straight away, you've got to take things gradually and persevere.

It's a really difficult balance for friends and family trying to offer support. On the one hand, there is the 'she'll snap out of it' attitude and, on the other, going completely over the top and focusing on you every second of the day looking for symptoms. It's a sensitive area because what you need seems to change.

People around you doing things, taking that bit of stress off can help enormously. Things like having the kids for the night so that my husband and I could have some time alone. Or cooking a meal, as I couldn't even face going into the kitchen. It's better if they offer to do it and don't have to be asked, because when you're depressed you haven't got the energy to ask.

It's those practical things that are so important, because you're getting your emotional support elsewhere and you're getting your therapeutic needs met through your psychiatrist. It's the day-to-day activities that need to be simplified, to take that hassle out of your daily routine. Friends came round when I first had my baby because there was an understanding that you would feel absolutely shattered – it's the same feeling when you are depressed.

When you're mentally sick, you need the same sort of support as if you are physically sick. You want someone to be a good mother, somebody to take you by the hand and take care of everything. I think husbands often find that difficult because it is a mothering role.

I would have to say again that the understanding that it is an illness was the most important thing. Once my husband had read an article on post-natal depression he was able to say, "Oh, that's exactly how you were." So it wasn't just a matter of me not coping. I think stigma is another big thing – if only people could get away from seeing being depressed as being crazy. People seem to brand you for life and what I don't like is that if you get sick in the future, people will say, "Oh well, she's been depressed before, it must be that," whereas if people saw it as an illness they would understand that once you've been treated, you're better. I think it's an awful stigma to have in the current climate.

I didn't want to tell my family because of the possible assumption that it was a marriage problem. People do see it that way – even my husband was seeing it that way at first, whereas it wasn't that at all. Problems were happening in the marriage because of the depression.

THINGS TO BE AWARE OF

In the telling of her story, Wendy has raised a number of important issues:

1

Different people have different levels of functioning. If your loved one has always been highly efficient and good at putting on a brave face, the likelihood is that she will continue to try. Because people appear to be coping, it doesn't mean that they are.

2

The convalescent period is a lengthy one, and you need to psychologically prepare

3

Although you may be suffering as a consequence, the depression is not aimed at you, and it is not because of you, so try not to personalise mood swings.

4

Part of the hesitation to come forward and offer support can be based on the misunderstanding that the problem is marital and hence respect for privacy should prevail. As a friend or extended family member, try to clarify this point rather than remain distant because of false assumptions.

5

Assistance in very practical ways will ease some of the stresses of daily living. This applies to friends and extended family members as well as partners.

CHAPTER 9

Husbands Matter Too

MYSTIFIED? I don't blame you if you are. After all, you gave up playing squash every Tuesday night for six months to go to antenatal classes, you overcame your fear of the sight of blood to be there at the birth, and now, a month after the birth, your wife's totally disinterested in you and the baby.

In the previous chapter I provided a clinical explanation of this phenomenon, (if you haven't read this, it would pay to flick back before continuing). I would now like to concentrate on the effects that this may be having on you as the partner and baby's father, (as there is now research being conducted that is showing that father's may also become depressed at this time) as well as offer further suggestions on how to handle the situation.

Once the depression has been diagnosed, the focus of treatment is on the mother. Practitioners are concerned with the infant's safety around the mother, and fathers do tend to be overlooked in this process. From a psychological perspective, you will be going through a period of considerable change. Even before the depression, you will have been faced with significant changes in your relationship, baby being the main focus. You will have had very little time together, intimacy replaced by fatigues and late-night feeds. You are not out of the ordinary if you feel very isolated during this time.

During the onset of the depressive illness, you will have undoubtedly been feeling more estranged and unloved, and, with the diagnosis, alienated and powerless. You may also have noticed that if you do withdraw because you are feeling unwanted, you quickly get the feeling that you are making things worse. Feeling stuck?

The next story is from a man who has experienced all of this but, I would like to introduce Rachel, his partner, and then have John take you through his journey as a husband and father dealing with post-natal depression.

Rachel's Story

This was my first child, a pregnancy that was very planned and, I thought, completely prepared for. However, after a couple of weeks, I became very lacking in motivation and not really connected. I don't remember much about what happened, and in fact I can't even remember Benjamin when he was very young. I never remember cooing and gooing. I used to think that John was pretending to like him so much, because I didn't.

All I knew was that I wanted to spend more time with John, but felt ambivalent about everything. I find it very easy to put on a face for people, so many people didn't know what I was feeling. Then I started to get frightened about what I was thinking and feeling, like I wanted to put something over our son's face or I would imagine dropping him. It was the scariest time in my life.

Once I had spoken about those feelings, I went to our GP and he referred me on to a psychiatrist. I didn't like the thought of going to a psychiatrist, but once I had, I was so relieved to find out that there was a reason for how I was feeling. I started to feel that I was going to be all right. The best thing I remember was when my psychiatrist said to me, "Everybody gets better from post-natal depression." That gave me something to hang on to, because otherwise I thought I was going out of my mind. I would rather have done myself in than live like that forever.

I really felt that I needed my family to help while I was waiting for the pills to kick in. Unfortunately, I had bad side-effects from the first lot of medication and started to experience panic attacks. After the change of medication, things started to get a lot better and, after five months of sitting like a blob, I started to come back to normal.

Looking back, there were certain things that were really helpful and other things that I feel should have been handled very differently. For instance, I really felt that the visiting nurse or midwife should have been able to recognise what was happening. I felt very influenced by what they thought about me as a mother.

I didn't and I don't think other people understand that it is a problem of chemical imbalance. I wished there had been more information and support groups, so that I could have learned about what it was and been able to listen to how other mothers felt. It makes me terrified when I imagine that I could have hurt my child before I knew what I was doing.

You want your friends and family to help with the day-to-day things – to help your partner by cooking a meal or looking after the baby. Friends and family really do need to support your partner, as it is very frightening to see someone you love depressed.

John's Perspective

As soon as Rachel told me about her thoughts, I started to get concerned and not long after took her to see our GP. Rachel woke up one morning and said she wanted to hurt Benjamin. She didn't say those exact words, "I want to hurt him". She said, "I've just been thinking what would happen if... I'd like to drop him on the floor just to see what would happen to him." I had to go out that morning and I found that I didn't feel comfortable leaving Benjamin with Rachel.

I had been noticing for a few days that Rachel was becoming more and more stressed and I felt that the visiting nurses were making things worse, pressuring her instead of trying to get her to relax. I also felt that they were insinuating that I was the problem, that I was the reason Rachel was feeling doubtful and tearful.

I came home from work one day, when Benjamin was two weeks

old, and Rachel had been sitting on the couch with him on her lap for four hours. She said that she didn't know how to settle him or what to do with him. I have children from a previous marriage, so I took care of things on that day.

I rang our doctor and he came to see Rachel. He suggested that she should go into a private hospital, but I wanted her to see a psychiatrist first and try to manage things from home. I felt strongly that if somebody is depressed and you take them out of their regular environment, you're cutting them off and it adds to the pressure, especially given the stigma that's attached to depression.

Rachel had never been in hospital before and I felt that it would actually impinge on her getting better. I suggested that we keep Rachel at home and try to have as normal a life as possible.

One of the things that I tried to do throughout all of this was to get a sense of normality around the home. Rachel was incapable of doing this. People would ring and she wouldn't remember if she'd hung up on them or what she had said to them if they came to the house.

Rachel got to the stage where she didn't want to leave the house. Previously she had led a very active professional and social life. I used to try and take her out as much as possible and show her that there was nothing to be afraid of. She used to worry about things she'd read in books, like you weren't able to take a baby to a supermarket for two months because they would breathe in germs.

I tried to be there and do the best I could, but I didn't feel that there were many resources to draw upon. We were left sitting between weekly appointments with the psychiatrist. There needed to be some form of education and ongoing support. I'm sure that there are a lot of women out there like Rachel, who don't even know they are suffering the symptoms. Women seem to say, "Well this is to be expected, it's part of having a baby, all women get blue and they just snap out of it and get on with life."

We relied on talking to as many people as we could. I encouraged Rachel to talk about it rather than hide it from everybody, making it something to be afraid of. I wanted her to be able to say, "Hey, I'm suffering from this illness and I just need you to bear with me for a while." The other thing was that Rachel used to find that talking about it would help her feel better.

In very practical terms, I took over a lot of Benjamin's care. I would comfort him often, and I used to feel that he could sense that there was something wrong. At night I would have him close to my side of the bed. If he started to cry, I'd hold my hand on his back and calm him down, and by doing so would take the pressure off Rachel, so that she wouldn't feel that every time he cried she would have to react.

Admittedly I did take a lot of time off work, and spending time at home meant that my work did suffer, but I felt that it was more important to be with Rachel, to make sure that she had some security. I knew that Rachel wanted me to be with her and would make the extra effort to be there.

We had a friend stay for a few days, but she couldn't cope with Rachel's depression. Other people's reactions amazed me. It was as though they were thinking, "Well you look all right physically, so you should be acting accordingly. You're just being a stupid child. Just get over it and grow up." It was the same with Rachel's mother. We couldn't tell her because her attitude was, "Look, I've had eight children, what the hell's the matter with you?"

I suppose the main thing that I did was to keep the house running. I did the shopping and the washing, I took Benjamin for walks, and when he needed to be fed I would take him to Rachel. He was being breastfed then and after Rachel had fed him I would bath him and settle him down, but I'd also try to make sure Rachel was involved as well.

I'd also try to create time for Rachel to do things that she enjoyed. I'd come home from work at lunch time and sit in the car with Benjamin whilst Rachel went for a swim and a relax on the beach. Or I'd stay at home with Benjamin while Rachel went off and did other things.

RACHEL: I have to interrupt here a minute and make the point that John ran himself ragged. It would have been great if there had been a group to contact to give him a break. I know now that if I had a friend in a similar situation I would go round and do the washing and the cooking, and make sure that the husband wasn't totally worn out from working and worrying about his wife and baby.

JOHN: Looking back, even simple things like getting a prescription filled were difficult, because I couldn't leave the house. In the very early stages, the psychiatrist wanted someone to be with Rachel 24-hours-a-day. I also felt that I needed to get away and step outside of things before I exploded.

I think that what's needed is someone who can explain and counsel the family through what is happening. To say, "These behaviours and responses are to be expected, you will go through these different stages, and there will be highs and lows."

Education and community support need to include a wider field, for example, in-laws or parents, so that they can get involved and form a family-based support group. Husbands aren't always the most equipped in the family to deal with illness, and beside, you still need to be able to step out for five minutes and recharge your batteries, no matter how much you love your wife. At times you start to think that you're going mad yourself, because you can't see any way through it. This is especially so before the illness is diagnosed.

You can go on for a long time knowing that things are wrong and not knowing what to do or what to say. Although I was able to respond to Rachel's cues, like being quiet and not talking, or asking her what she was thinking, it took a long time for her to admit that she wanted to hurt Benjamin.

RACHEL: In fact the only way I could tell John how I was feeling was by keeping a diary. I used to write really angry and horrible things, but it helped me. I also knew that if I left the diary lying somewhere, John would know I wanted him to read it. There were things that I just couldn't verbalise because I felt too terrible about them, or was just too emotional. That way John always knew what I was feeling and it helped me to stop worrying as much.

JOHN: Once she had started to open up to me, I wanted to let her know that she wasn't going to be punished for telling me those things. I wanted her to be able to trust me.

This is again where the educational aspect is so important. I needed her to trust that I wasn't going to grab the phone, have her committed and keep the baby from her. That was something I never did. I never kept the baby away from Rachel, never physically separated them. I tried hard not to panic. When I did get stressed, I would talk to people and tell them what was happening. In fact, I know at times I would talk about it whether they wanted to listen to me or not.

GWENDOLINE: You spoke earlier about being disappointed with some of the support from visiting nurses, how did you find other professional support services?

JOHN: There were times when I felt that the psychiatrist really hadn't explained things to me all that well, given that I was the main support person. This was especially the case with information about Rachel's medication. Rachel had this thing in her mind that she wanted to come off the medication after a six-month period. I would try to say to Rachel that there was no pressure to come off the medication and that she should stop when she didn't need to take it any more.

I explained to the psychiatrist that I thought it was happening too quickly, and sure enough, she went downhill fast. She started sitting around again feeling tearful and depressed. I feel Rachel really went backwards during that period of time. I felt that I should have been consulted as to what I could see, rather than just believing Rachel. Perhaps they could say something like, "If you start feeling that she's going backwards, or starting to display symptoms of depression again, this is what you should do." I felt the medical support should have been a little more cautious and inclusive.

Being informed of what to expect would have been helpful as well, so as not to be caught completely by surprise. You might think that the person is getting better, so you need to know that they could drop back from time to time – a couple of steps forward and a few backwards. You need to know that it's not necessarily anything that you've done, or not done, it's just that that's part of the deal – the person will have up days and really down days without any tangible thing that you can see having caused it.

GWENDOLINE: All this must have placed a great deal of strain on the marriage.

JOHN: There's almost an expectation, an inevitability, that the marriage won't survive. We heard stories from a support group, where out of seven couples there were only two couples still together after a period of three months. Both Rachel and I felt that there was not enough understanding of what was happening and hence not enough support from the husbands in particular – it became an excuse to walk away.

GWENDOLINE: A great fear for the depressed mother is that because she feels so unattractive and worthless, has no interest in life and certainly no interest in sex, she can't blame her partner for going out and having an affair. In fact it occurs to me that significant attention needs to be paid to a couple's level of intimacy for the survival of the relationship. A little old-fashioned comment like, "I still love you" is a very tangible way of providing reassurance.

JOHN: Another very practical suggestion that I would have for husbands is to not "buy in". Rachel would try to bait me with comments – it was almost like she wanted to create an argument over something because she was feeling down. A lot of it was out of frustration and her low sense of self-worth. It was important for me not to buy into it, to just realise what was going on and step back.

The only other thing I would add, which I think is really important, is to discuss things like post-natal depression in the ante-natal classes, so you're even a little bit prepared. The focus tends to be too much on the positive things. I think there should be a lot more emphasis on all the issues involved in having a child, and this education should include the husband as well as the mother.

IN A NUTSHELL

There will be times when you feel alienated and despondent. Try not to take things personally and make sure that you develop a support system for yourself.

Don't be afraid to talk to others about how you are feeling – it helps and it also begins to destigmatise the illness, so you're not left feeling that you are a bad husband.

Be assertive with health professionals. Request that you are involved and are kept informed of any changes in medication or major clinical decision-making.

Follow your instincts. If you feel that your partner is getting worse, or is coming off the medication too soon, express your opinion.

In very severe cases, as with post-natal psychosis, it may be best for your partner to be hospitalised. This does not mean you have failed. It is a matter of what is best for her and the baby at this time.

Your help is valuable in the most practical ways – helping with chores around the house, cooking meals, bathing baby, doing the shopping. Try to involve your partner in these tasks, especially if they involve the baby.

Inform people at work what is going on, so that you can perhaps leave work a little early or take time off when needed.

Encourage your partner to talk about how she is feeling and try not to be judgemental about the unpleasant thoughts she may reveal.

Try to provide a 'buffer' for your partner, as friends and family members may not understand what she is going through and may become critical.

Keep visits from friends and family at a moderate level. Large social gatherings are not advisable.

Organise breaks for both for you – short walks, time away from the house.

Get up to the baby at night, and try to let your partner sleep through, minimising sleep disturbance.

Don't forget to say, "I love you".

CHAPTER 10

More than Just a phase

AS SOON AS your child, no matter what the age, does anything that appears a little 'unusual', other knowing parents, grandparents, books on raising children, all inform you that "it's just a phase". Remember back to when you couldn't sit quietly on the loo reading an outdated magazine without the door being thrown open by an assertive two-year-old? Specialists assure you that it's "separation anxiety – part of establishing the ego boundary, part of the transition from the infantile state of narcissistic omnipotence". Your parents remind you what a brat you were at that age and your friends tell you about the 'terrible twos', the consensus being, "There's nothing to worry about, it's just a phase."

And there are many phases, many different stages of development. Accompanying each developmental milestone are moments of great joy – the first word, the first step, the first school report card. But there are also times of distress, rage, and panic – the first time the school calls to say your child has been suspended, the first time the police brings him home, the first time she screams, "I hate you and I want to kill myself!"

Adolescence, the phase that no one could prepare you for, is in fact a developmental stage that is considered to be a comparatively recent phenomenon. They've never heard of it in Papua New Guinea – one minute you're a boy child, and then you get beaten about the back with a hand-made cane implement, bleed a bit and, as long as you don't cry, you become a man. During the Industrial Revolution, children working alongside adults in a cotton mill or a coal mine would have clearly defined roles and expectations. In our society, this has all changed – childhood and adulthood have been pushed further apart, and in that gap exists adolescence.

The changes have occurred both biologically and environmentally. Improvements in childhood health and nutrition are said to have contributed to the shift in onset of puberty from around 18 or 19 years-of-age to a mean of 13 to 15 years-of-age. Children now grow much bigger earlier in life, hence adult-like bodies and physical capacities occur much sooner than before. Unfortunately, this increased interest in and capacity for sexuality at a much younger age has not been accompanied by acceleration in emotional and social development.

At the same time as the onset of puberty, adolescents often have to change school and, perhaps, peer group. The marketing machine plays on their insecurity of being in limbo between child and adulthood, rocketing them further into the land of designer labels and acne creams. Employment opportunities are based on higher levels of educational attainment, requiring them to live at home longer, leaving them economically dependent on their parents for longer periods to time. Genetically we were designed to leave home once sexually mature, reducing the risk of inbreeding and forcing the adolescent to seek relationships outside of the home.

The traditional roles and expectations for children and adults are now different, but undefined, resulting in confusion for both adolescents and their parents. As a result of social realities such as economic dependence and decreased employment opportunities, young adults may experience exaggerated feelings of helplessness. Their frustrated attempts at achieving autonomy often lead to hopelessness and despair, both emotions that can provide a perfect host environment for depression. International research cites depression in epidemic proportions and also alerts us to the trend toward more depression at a younger age – a trend verified by the increase in teenage suicide rates.

Is it just that Black is a Fashion Statement?

Something that often bewilders parents of teenagers is how to make the differentiation between 'a phase they're going through', 'it's in fashion', 'all their friends are doing it' or something more. Their clothes are black, their music sounds black, and every time you won't let them use the car, their mood turns black. So how is it possible to detect depression in your teenager, when so much of the behaviour looks like ordinary teenage, sloth-like behaviour? Are they sleeping a lot because they talk all night on the phone and are in the middle of another growth spurt, or is it a symptom of depression?

The following is the symptom checklist we referred to in Chapter One, modified to incorporate adolescent idiosyncrasies. *Remember:* If at least four of the following symptoms have been present nearly every day for a period of two weeks or more, you need a professional opinion.

1. Changes in weight or appetite

Adolescent eating patterns are difficult to assess, particularly with teenage girls dieting and the prevalence of eating disorders. Look out for the stopping of regular meals and changes in body weight of more than 5 per cent per month.

2. Constantly complaining of being bored, hating school

It is important to be aware of any marked changes in school performance – failing exams, refusing to go to school, etc.

3. Feelings of sadness

These feelings last most of the day and nearly every day. Constant irritability or tearfulness is marked with adolescents.

4. Thoughts of death or suicide

Talking about death, only ever listening to depressing music; idolising cult figures who have taken their lives; suicide attempts; a specific plan of how they would commit suicide.

5. Feeling guilty, hopeless or worthless

Over-concern with the state of the world; thinking everything is meaningless. Preoccupation with the world coming to an end, nuclear wars, world tragedy.

6. Changes in sleeping pattern

They could be watching television all night because they can't sleep, or in bed asleep all day because they can't face the world.

7. Inability to concentrate, remember things, or make decisions

This also manifests itself in changes in performance at school – as their concentration span decreases, so does their ability to achieve academically.

8. Fatigue or loss of energy.

9. Loss of interest in the opposite sex.

10. Loss of interest or pleasure in activities once enjoyed.

This is especially important when it involves becoming isolated from friends. Adolescents may do a lot of very annoying things but they usually do them with their friends. This cutting off from their peer group is one of the most important indicators.

In addition, depressive illness with adolescents is often accompanied by tobacco, alcohol and drug abuse (most teenagers will experiment – it is ongoing abuse that needs to be addressed); promiscuous sexual behaviour and risk-taking behaviour, for example, driving cars when intoxicated.

Depression may also follow bereavement, particularly if there is a family history of depression. Other severe stressors include physical or sexual assault. With a family history of depression, the risk is increased.

There is consistent evidence from a wide range of international studies that suggests young people who have psychiatric illnesses are at increased risk of suicidal behaviour. The most common psychiatric disorders include depression, substance abuse/dependence, and personality and adjustment disorders. Over half of those studied have 'comorbid' (ie. two or more) psychiatric diagnoses.

The initial onset of schizophrenic illness, which also occurs in mid to late adolescence, can present in very similar ways to depression. This is why I encourage psychiatric assessment if you are concerned about the mental well-being of your child.

Another theme that emerges in the research is the increased risk of suicidal behaviour in young people with poor self-esteem and aggressive or antisocial traits. Poor parent/child relationships, family dysfunction, family breakdowns are all identified as risk factors.

It should also be noted that puberty is a time for increased sexual awareness and issues to do with sexuality. Being sensitive to conflict with regards sexual preference is essential. Young males, in particular, struggling with homosexuality can be very vulnerable to depression. They are even more at risk if they are in schools or family environments where they could be fearful about the possible responses of their families and/or peers.

The above information is designed to help you make that important differentiation between a depressed teenager and a 'normal' teenager. Once the diagnosis has been made, the next important step is providing you with skills and understanding to help you cope, as parents and as a family.

Types of Help

Essentially there are four components to psychiatric/psychological intervention:

1. PSYCHOEDUCATION

This is education involving all aspects of depressive illness and treatment strategies. Wherever possible this should include the entire family. All family members are affected by living with a depressed person, and discussions that promote understanding of the illness do serve to ease tension within the family environment.

Information about symptoms and early signs of recurrence of the illness will enable you and your family to seek further treatment and help prevent relapse.

2. PHARMACOTHERAPY (MEDICATION)

When a medication is prescribed, ask for specific information on the choice of drug, and its effect and benefits. If the family understands the purpose of the medication, safeguards are being put in place to make sure it is being taken as prescribed. (Don't forget, you haven't got eyes in the back of your head.)

Involvement of brothers and sisters is essential to avoid collusion in treatment-resistant behaviour. They are obviously concerned about what is happening, and may not like the idea of their sibling being on 'drugs', and may encourage non-compliance out of naivete.

3. HOSPITALISATION

Inpatient treatment should be reserved for those who are psychotic, acutely suicidal, or continuously abusing substances and putting themselves and others at great risk. In other words, those who cannot be managed at home. To feel comfortable with this decision, you should discuss it in great depth with the psychiatrist. Wherever possible, adolescents should be hospitalised in adolescent units, not in adult ones. This may involve travelling to a major metropolitan centre, but most families report that it is worth the extra effort.

4. PSYCHOTHERAPY

Family therapy is a valuable tool in the treatment of adolescent depression. Sessions should be aimed at resolving conflicts within the family, particularly where other issues such as substance abuse, divorce, family or personal trauma for the adolescent are involved.

Family therapy sessions can also provide an arena for the family to discuss and attempt to resolve the tension and frustrations that are a direct result of the depressive symptomatology. I'm going to hand the explanation of this statement over to someone who has been in this very position.

Julie's Story

We were probably able to recognise the signs because my mother-in-law has suffered from depression. It seemed to start whilst my son Steven was working on a particular science project. He had just turned seventeen. He would be awake at 3 o'clock in the morning trying to complete it, but seemed to be coping with the rest of his school work. However, as things developed he became increasingly obsessed, and I believe worked so hard he burnt himself out.

He would arrive home, never say, "hello". He'd go to his room, go straight to bed and pull the blankets over his head. He wasn't even interested in coming down from his room to have dinner. He has always been a quiet boy, but this was too extreme. He insisted there was nothing wrong with him and we insisted on taking him to the doctor. He was diagnosed with depression.

I immediately felt guilty and thought, "what have I done to have my child in this state?" The doctor then told me that he had suicidal tendencies, and I really couldn't come to terms with that. When I first took him to the doctor, I thought everything would be fixed in a month, that he just needed something to snap him out of it. I never expected it to be something that would take over the next eight months of our lives.

The drug he was prescribed didn't work for him, and he spent the whole Christmas holidays drifting around home doing absolutely nothing. He didn't want to go anywhere or do anything, he just sat watching television. His friends had told us prior to the school holidays that he had been wandering around the playground by himself, even standing in the rain oblivious of everybody.

Things became complicated for us, because Steven went through a period of going high, and he also started to experience panic attacks. I remember one occasion when the whole family went to the movies. We were all seated, when Steven stood up and said, "I can't stay here." My husband was trying to keep things calm, and his sister Jane was saying, "He's such a nuisance, doing this to us again." She thought he was just being obtuse.

So the medications had to be changed again and lithium was introduced. Steven wasn't keen to go on lithium because it would make his skin bad and of course this resulted in all sorts of self-esteem problems. We also found out at this time that there was an infatuation involved, unfortunately unrequited love, and this wasn't helping either.

Steven became extremely unwell and had to be taken out of school. We utilised a school that was part of the Mental Health Services, to keep him safe during the day and allow us to get on with our lives. When we felt he had improved enough, he came home. He would still take things out on us when he was at home, which made it difficult.

Our friends were wonderfully supportive. They would call us regularly and invite us out, knowing that we needed a break from what was happening at home. Not all of our immediate family were understanding: I think a lot of them thought Steven was putting it on.

Talking to a woman whose daughter has bipolar disorder was also a great help. She suggested I move back a little from Steven and try not to take everything on board. She made me aware that he also had to try to get himself well, and I couldn't fix everything, no matter how hard I tried. I met this woman quite by coincidence when I was out walking. I was so pleased, as I really wanted to talk to another mother.

I had tried to find a support group of some kind, but was told there was nothing for Steven's age group. I was really desperate at the time. When it's happening, you think that it's never going to end.

GWENDOLINE: Would you have considered having Steven committed and treated with ECT?

JULIE: I didn't want Steven to have ECT, but if he had become worse I'd have had to do it. I mean, you just can't carry on with somebody like that forever, it's not fair on the rest of the family, it really isn't. In fact, it's made our youngest child grow up rather more quickly than he would have otherwise, but he was very caring and understanding. I think he saw how much it hurt my husband and me, because it's very hurtful when you're trying to communicate with somebody who is totally oblivious and not in the slightest bit interested.

You know you're just up against a brick wall the whole time and it is quite soul destroying. You are just helpless until that person wants to communicate.

Steven's sister, who no longer lives at home, tried to communicate by writing to him. I thought she might be able to influence him, but she couldn't either. She tried very hard to be patient, but she's not a naturally patient person. She would say to me, "Mum, you kowtow to him too much. Give him a rocket occasionally, make him sit up and take notice. He gets all the attention in this house!" I tried to explain to her that yelling at him wasn't going to help. But I did get very cross with what I perceived to be his very selfish attitude. We would try to involve him in everything – trips away, shopping – but nothing seemed to work.

Then I started to notice that he was different with his friends than he was with the family at home, and I started to wonder if he was getting better but was playing games with the family. I talked to his friends about how he was at school and I found that a very good guideline as to how he was.

He had been going to a counsellor, and she had given him a book that she wanted him to write in every day. I had been very careful about not asking him what he talked about or what he was writing, as I felt that it was a private affair, but I thought, "Damn this, this is the whole family being affected by this blasted performance."

So I looked at what he had been writing and I found that the counsellor had not been getting an honest picture of what was going on at home. Steven was making it look as though we didn't involve him in anything.

We were not included much in his therapy and, when we were, they were joint sessions with Steven. The biggest hassle was that when we were all together, I didn't feel that I could say how I was feeling without thinking that I was betraying Steven by saying things in front of him. I felt I could never be totally honest, whereas if I'd had a couple of sessions with the counsellor, without Steven, I would have felt that she was seeing both points of view.

What was really helpful, though, was having her explain what was going on in Steven's head. That he wasn't able to make decisions, that he wasn't just being ignorant when he wouldn't engage in conversations. She explained things in a way that did make sense to me, and if she hadn't explained them it would never have occurred to me. I thought he was just being damned difficult and wanted to know why.

GWENDOLINE: The hard thing, of course, is that teenagers can be difficult at the best of times, and it is a very real clinical challenge to determine where the illness starts and finishes and what is purely behavioural or a function of their personality.

What to Do

1. BE THERE TO LISTEN

People who feel sad need to have their feelings acknowledged by those close to them. If the 'snap out of it' approach or simply ignoring the problem worked, there wouldn't be a need to develop treatments for depression.

2. ENCOURAGE THEM TO OPEN UP

You may need to invent creative ways of getting your loved one to talk to you, but it's important that you know how he is feeling. This is especially important if he has expressed suicidal intent. If you don't communicate, you'll find yourself snooping through diaries and trying to vet phone calls.

3. WHAT MAKES HER FEEL GOOD?

Try to find out the things that she does still enjoy and instigate these things. For instance, taking a long bath, going swimming, eating ice-cream. These things can be used as distractions.

4. WHO DOES HE TALK TO?

Often adolescents will talk to anybody except their parents. Don't interfere with this; in fact encourage your child to talk to others. However, do make it clear, particularly to his friends, that you must know if he is thinking about or planning a suicide attempt.

5. ENSURE HER SAFETY

One of the most important things right now is that your child is safe. Clear medicine cupboards of pills or medications that could be used to overdose. Remove any firearms from the home.

6. HELP HIM MAKE DECISIONS

He may be struggling with the simplest of decisions, such as what to wear that day. Help him organise his daily activities. He may not be able to ask for help, so you need to take the initiative.

7. BE A LITTLE INTRUSIVE IF YOU HAVE TO

Clearly you do not want your child mixing with friends who could be abusing substances and are ignorant of the circumstances, so try and monitor social contact, if there is any. If she is totally withdrawn, try to organise contact with friends. Make telephone contact with them during the day.

8. DON'T BE TOO FRIGHTENED TO ASK

Talking and asking questions about your child's suicidal thoughts will be scary for you, but it is better that you know.

9. DON'T FORGET OTHER FAMILY MEMBERS

Because your depressed child is your main focus at this point in time, other children will be going through times of feeling left out and will perhaps feel a little resentful. They need to be acknowledged and kept informed of what is happening.

10. GET INVOLVED

Of course you want to respect your teenager's privacy, but request to be kept informed by health professionals. Insist upon both joint and individual sessions. Involve the rest of the family when necessary.

11. DON'T FORGET YOURSELF

You have a life as well. Make sure you are taking time out and taking car of the care-giver.

...& WHAT NOT TO DO

1

Blame yourself.

2

Feel guilty.

3

Go to sleep at night thinking, "Where did I go wrong?"

CHAPTER 11

Why wouldn't I be depressed

"If your favourite grandmother had died,
If your best friend had moved away,
And your dog had died,
Your parents had divorced
And you got bullied when you went to work,
How would you feel?"
Quote from a child 2001

I THINK you and I both know how we would feel, very sad and very, very unhappy (to say the least) and if we stayed that way for a period of time, there is a high probability that we would become depressed. Yet it doesn't seem to occur to us that children could suffer from depression.

Ever heard yourself say, *"Oh to be a child again. Children are so resilient, they just bounce back."*

Or what about this one, *"Have you met Mary and Bob's little boy, funny child, miserable all the time, just a miserable sort of child I suppose. Some children are just like that."*

Another favourite of mine is *"It's just a phase, they go through at this age."*

Up until very recently it would have been unheard for an adult to consider that Mary and Bob's little boy could in fact be clinically depressed. In fact there wasn't even an official diagnosis for childhood depression until 1980. Here again, I was reminded of my own oversight, having not written a chapter on this phenomenon in the first edition of this book, *Sharing the Load*. An oversight, which I now perceive as reflective of the attitudes of society at large. Hence, my research into this chapter has been another personal learning curve.

I was intrigued to discover – (and I think you'll also find this story interesting) – the origins of significant research into depression in children in the late 1950's.

> A young paediatrician by the name of Leon Cytryn, was struck by the frequency of sadness and withdrawal in boys admitted to hospital for surgery on their undescended testicles. He began to explore the emotional adjustment of these boys, discovering that almost half had symptoms, that would have been associated with adult depression; feelings of hopelessness, sad mood etc. He continued his research through into the 1960's, and found many physically ill children to be markedly depressed. But Cytryn and another colleague McKnew were aware that a diagnosis of childhood depression was not acceptable to the medical profession. Medical teaching still insisted that children did not become depressed in a clinical sense. When McKnew tried to elicit help from other disciplines to study the biochemistry, no one was willing to cooperate, at that time the notion of childhood depression was deemed preposterous. (Cytryn & McKnew, 1996)

So what is the problem?

My theory goes something like this; people are still sceptical although somewhat more accepting of adult depression but when it comes to children, there are still those beliefs that go something like this:

"The only people benefiting from all this talk about depression are the drug companies and now they want to make money out of children, it's outrageous."

"If they just got on with their lives and got over it, they'd grow up stronger."

"They put all that money and effort into looking for all these conditions, that's half the problem, they start to find things that aren't there."

In fairness, there is a small element of truth in some of these scepticisms. There is widespread discussion amongst clinicians and academics as to whether or not the increase in the incidence of childhood and/or adult depression is a result of the ever-increasing pressures and stress within our society, or is it due to the more sophisticated methods of diagnosis and the wider acceptance. The jury is still out on that one, but there is no longer a debate as to the existence of depressive disorders in children.

The other part of the mythology has to do with, **just get on with it grow up and grow stronger**. As science advances, researchers become more clear and more definitive about stating that "early onset depression is highly predictive of adult problems" In a nutshell depressed children are more likely to become depressed adults. I wish I had a dollar for every time one of my adult clients said to me, *"When I really think about it, I don't even remember being happy as a child."*

So how as a parent can you know if your child is depressed or at risk of being depressed? As clinicians it is not our intent to alarm parents or to suggest that if a child feels sad about their grandmother dying or their cat getting run over by a car, that you should rush off to the doctor. However a main point to remember is that where: **sadness is a normal and healthy response when your child is upset, there comes a time when it is no longer appropriate to the loss or stress and your child is at risk of developing a serious emotional problem such as a depression or an anxiety disorder.**

In this next section I'm going to condense a mammoth amount of information on childhood depression from two wonderful child psychiatrists (Dr. C. Immelman and Professor J. Werry) and books written by some of the world's leading specialists, into a practical and accessible format to help guide you through this unknown territory.

REMEMBER

You know your own child best, it will be you that observes the changes in behaviour and emotion

Check with other sources that know your child well, such as teachers and school counsellors. Particularly given the role that bullying can play in childhood depression.

Trust your instincts, when you have made sure there are no physical causes, and you still feel something is wrong consult a mental health professional. (Wherever possible someone with a specialist interest in children's mental health issues.)

IS YOUR CHILD DEPRESSED? – A CHECKLIST

- Irritability, low tolerance for frustration.
- Loss of pleasure in previously enjoyed activities.
- Frequent feelings of sadness.
- Overactivity or excessive restlessness.
- Frequent unexplained stomach aches, headaches and fatigue.
- Weight loss or failure to achieve expected weight gain (less frequently excessive weight gain).
- Consistent verbal expressions of sadness and hopelessness, such as "I'll never feel happy again".
- Evidence of low self-esteem – "the other kids at school are really bright, no one likes me".
- Frequent and excessive worrying, assuming that something bad is going to happen, that it will be a catastrophe. The family will get hurt.
- Changes in sleep patterns. Difficulty falling asleep, waking in the middle of the night, or alternatively oversleeping and wanting to sleep during the day.
- Refusal or reluctance to go to school
- A marked drop in school performance, where previously they have been doing well.
- Little interest in playing with their friends
- Decreased energy, often looking tired and moving slowly.
- Communication becomes difficult, speaking almost becomes too much of an effort.
- Repeated thoughts about or attempts to run away from home.
- Unprovoked hostility or aggression, refusing to do things, fights at school
- Excessive tearfulness or frequently feeling like they want to cry.
- Morbid or suicidal thoughts, frequent fantasies of death and dying, repeated themes of death in drawings.

A special note: No one symptom in this list equates to a diagnosis of depression or a clinically significant emotional problem. However ANY indication of suicidal thoughts or behaviour, must be taken seriously, regardless of frequency. If this happens your child is in immediate need of professional help.

There are also other conditions that can have similar symptoms and certainly have links to depression; such as Attention Deficit Hyperactivity Disorder (ADHD), Post Traumatic Stress Disorder (PTSD), learning disabilities and the anxiety disorders. Because of these overlays accurate diagnosis is essential.

In the first chapter of this book I have outlined the internationally accepted clinical symptoms of depression, I have also made note that in order for a diagnosis to be made symptoms need to have been in existence for more than two weeks. Depressed children, will often not experience their symptoms consistently they may come and go frequently and over a period of time. To be a symptom of depression these behaviours should also be representative of a change from how your child usually behaves. *Help Me, I'm Sad* (Fassler & Dumas, Penguin 1997) is an extremely helpful book, providing you with a lot of additional information in this area.

In his book Dr David Fassler asks parents to concentrate on one key question when attempting to determine whether their child is truly depressed: "To what extent do your child's sad feelings and behaviour interfere with their everyday life and normal development?"

There are a number of measurement tools, that can be useful in helping you determines the answer to this question. The following inventory can be used in either of two ways. You can answer them yourself based on how you think they would answer, or for slightly older children sit down with them and go through the questions. Suggest that it was something you were wondering about.

THE CHOATE DEPRESSION INVENTORY FOR CHILDREN (CDIC)

[Answer TRUE or FALSE]

1. I feel sad a lot of the time. ☐ ☐
2. I have trouble sleeping. ☐ ☐
3. I feel tired a lot of the time. ☐ ☐
4. I don't have many friends. ☐ ☐
5. I cry a lot. ☐ ☐
6. I don't like playing with other kids. ☐ ☐
7. I don't feel as hungry as I used to. ☐ ☐
8. Other children don't like me. ☐ ☐
9. I feel lonely. ☐ ☐
10. I have lots of headaches and stomach aches. ☐ ☐
11. I don't like school. ☐ ☐
12. I have bad dreams. ☐ ☐
13. Sometimes I think about hurting myself. ☐ ☐
14. I worry a lot. ☐ ☐
15. I don't like myself. ☐ ☐
16. Other children have more fun than me. ☐ ☐
17. I don't do as well at school as I used to. ☐ ☐
18. Sometimes I have a lot of trouble concentrating. ☐ ☐
19. I feel angry a lot of the time. ☐ ☐
20. I get into a lot of fights. ☐ ☐

(NB. True for three or more items would warrant an evaluation by a professional. A 'true' answer for item 13 – self-destructive, suicidal thoughts – always necessitates an evaluation.)

David Fassler, 1997

Types of help

1. MEDICATION

There is still a lot of work to be done in the area of childhood depression particularly in relation to the efficacy of medications. Although clinicians agree that medication should not be the first treatment option, and should not be prescribed casually or lightly, it can be extremely helpful and life-saving particularly for children expressing suicidal thoughts. Also where medication proves to be the most helpful is where the symptoms have become largely physiological. Never allow your child to go on medication without a thorough medical check-up always being aware of similarity in symptoms with other conditions that for instance involve the thyroid function.

2. FAMILY THERAPY

The therapist works alongside the family. Helping them identify relationship issues or communication difficulties that maybe contributing to your child's depressed mood. There may have been a lot of stress in the family or a very significant death and with each family member coping with their own individual needs the communication links have broken down. A depressed child, maybe actually expressing some of the distress and symptoms of grief of the family. It is often the more sensitive children that will manifest their unhappiness in this way. This type of focussed family therapy is not to find blame in parenting skills, but is designed to develop more healthy ways of communicating particularly when there are problems the family is dealing with.

3. INDIVIDUAL THERAPY

Although family therapy can make a significant contribution, individual therapy for the child is also essential. The same types of therapy I have outlined earlier such as psychodynamic psychotherapy, cognitive behavioural therapy and interpersonal psychotherapy (See Chapter 4) are also used by the therapist when working with children

(i) Psychodynamic Psychotherapy

This form of therapy is often more effective with children than with adults. Using techniques such as painting or drawing, play therapy, encouraging fantasy play, with a very skilled therapist, can encourage communication in younger children. These methods are often far less threatening than direct questioning and listening techniques. I emphasise 'skilled' therapists as these techniques can be very open to interpretations of such phenomena as sexual abuse where this is not otherwise evidenced.

(ii) Cognitive Behavioural Therapy (CBT)

Depressed children, like adults will blame themselves when anything bad happens to them or their family. Children are even more prone to this because of the nature of childhood is to be very self-centred. Through CBT the therapist can identify the child's negative thinking patterns and the behaviours that contribute to these themes. They are then equipped to help them learn to re-evaluate what is happening in a more positive light and replace perhaps very self-defeating behaviours with more constructive and helpful ways of communicating their emotions.

HOSPITALISATION

In very extreme cases a child may need to be hospitalised. Care outside of the home is rarely suggested however, in cases where there is risk of suicide, consider this as an option.

These are a few but tend to be the more widely used therapeutic approaches. The books I have recommended will give you a far more in-depth understanding of the types of therapy. But whatever approach they chose all of the following guidelines will be helpful

- Work alongside your child's therapist
- Be prepared to go for sessions without your child learning how you can best assist.
- If programmes are recommended stick with the schedules, this is a priority.

- Keep the whole process as 'normalised' as possible
- Keep talking and listening

Most of all
Show lots of love and affection be encouraging.

When I began looking for a family to share their experience with you, clinicians I approached stated that when the ordeal was over for families, they just wanted to move on and not reflect or look back. That in looking back, they may have to experience revisiting a time so frightening and painful. However, I did manage to find one such family.

Jenny's Story

Jenny was twelve when she lost her brother, she loved him and loved him and yet he still got sick and he still died. No matter how good she was, and how much she prayed, he was taken from her. She was angry and she was sad. She was powerless and disillusioned and she understood nothing anymore about what was right and wrong. What was fair and just, and neither could she tell the world about her pain. All she knew was that the one she loved was taken from her and she was left with this ache that wouldn't go away and wouldn't go away and wouldn't go away. And then she got sick, and all she knew was that she was so sick she wanted to die.

From her father

Initially I was convinced that Jenny had contracted glandular fever or something viral and that it had coincided with the loss of her brother. She was lethargic, refused to get up out of bed; she had no appetite, no longer had contact with her friends and never went back to school.

She was never really a child that would talk about her feelings, although she would with her brother and when he was sick she spent every possible moment with him. We understood this and didn't want to push her but after her brother had gone, she became completely uncommunicative. She would sulk and want to stay in bed, she would walk around slamming doors but what she would complain about was "aching all over". When I look back I can see that it was the physical symptoms of depression, but at the time the possibility of a physical explanation such as a virus was still being considered and endless tests were being done. I feel that we wasted a lot of time with all the tests.

GWENDOLINE: How did you feel about the diagnosis of depression and the possible use of medication?

Father: When we finally got there, I believed the diagnosis was correct. I was sceptical of the medication and was worried that she would become dependent and would be on it for the rest of her life. Because of stories we had heard from people about antidepressants. We had been suggested St John's Wort but it made no difference at all. But she responded almost instantly and it was almost miraculous in the change it brought about. I remember her mother saying, "We have our daughter back".

GWENDOLINE: What would you have done differently if anything?

Father : Probably nothing, I tried many times to get her to talk about her sense of loss but she never would. But I know how much the loss has overwhelmed her and changed her. Prior to her brother becoming sick she was well-adjusted and doing exceptionally well at school, she was attentive and considered the 'model' student. She was also aware of her image, liking to look 'cool' always taking care of her appearance and wanting to wear all the latest labels and brands. She became uncaring about these aspects of her life. When she went to school her behaviour was disruptive and most notably she had become insecure. Since her depression has been treated these things are resolving themselves and she is maturing or at least seems to be more in line with the other kids

GWENDOLINE: What would you say to other parents?

Father : Don't push your children to do anything they don't want to and try to be aware as you can of all aspects of their health mental and physical. Children don't or maybe because they are young can't explain their feelings as adults do. Hence, all the physical symptoms. I am now convinced that Jenny's physical problems were all a part of the depression. It is hard to come to terms with the stigma that is associated with mental illness when dealing with these things. But I know we will always be mindful of Jenny's susceptibility to depression. Something I know we both have become more conscious of, is saying positive and supportive things to our children wherever we can.

Through her mother's eyes

It was a very confusing time for us because Jenny had lost her beloved brother and then became physically unwell with symptoms similar to glandular fever. The health professionals explained to us that to have suffered a traumatic emotional event and then get physically sick can increase the chances of a very severe depression. They explained to us the biological nature of depression, that it was a chemical imbalance and that her brain was having difficulty maintaining serotonin levels. That once treated with medication her brain would be able to function naturally again. I was most concerned that Jenny would become dependant on the drugs. The medication worked brilliantly, she eventually stopped taking them and there have been no problems since. As her parents we do still worry that she will always have an extra sensitivity to life's ups and downs.

GWENDOLINE: Did you feel at any time that Jenny felt so hopeless that maybe life for her didn't seem worth living

Mother: We tried to encourage her to talk about her feelings but even up until this day that is difficult. She was so angry with life when we would try and take her to appointments she would try and jump out of the car. When she wouldn't get out of bed I thought it was because she had this virus, I even had to push her to have a shower. She would lay on his bed feigning to sleep, she never even watched the TV. Luckily Harry Potter had just been released and I used to read to her for hours.

Finally I forced her to get up and have a bath, subconsciously my instincts were not to leave her alone. I now know why. While I left her in the bath for a moment I returned to find her quietly submerged under the water with no intention of coming up. I had to force her up above the water. When challenged with "What's wrong with you? – Don't you want to live?" she replied with a definite "NO"

It was in immediate response to this that we started the medication.

GWENDOLINE: After such a frightening experience, what words of warning would you give other parents?

Mother: We very much were doing things one day at a time, but fortunately the health professionals we were recommended acted quickly and kept us informed. With this illness it is essential that you deal with things swiftly and effectively. I'm sure natural therapists are well meaning but I feel that a lot of precious time can be wasted taking doses of the natural remedies. It makes me angry when people believe that chronic or severe conditions can be treated by often unverified natural therapies. In my opinion natural therapies work well for people who aren't severely unwell, like our daughter had become. Don't waste time, seek professional help immediately. "My advice to parents is that you know in your heart of hearts when your child is not behaving normally, don't ignore that feeling."

As I mentioned earlier in this chapter, childhood depression is such a novice concept for most of us, myself included. I most of all wanted you to gain some solace and understanding from this chapter. I do not believe I would have been able to achieve this in such a profound way without 'Jenny's Story'. To her family, I wish to express my respect and admiration for sharing this with me and gifting you with their insights – I hope this has helped.

CHAPTER 12

A Family Affair

NO MATTER how old your child is – sixteen or forty-six – if something is wrong, you're going to worry. If you're anything like my parents, you may never have come in contact with depressive illness before. In fact, my father stated in a somewhat bemused manner, "Makes you wonder, though, this depression – it must be something that's only just started. Because I'm 75 and I've never heard of it. I don't think my generation has ever heard of depression, it wasn't around in our day." Depression isn't new – talking openly about it is.

Depression is a 'family affair' and is best managed that way. You may have felt that your situation was totally unique and that perhaps

you are to blame. You're not. This chapter is your opportunity to learn from the hindsight of other families and gain solace from their understanding.

A Mother's Recollections

With both my step-son and my own daughter, I found that they were not actually able to participate in family things. It was hard to just get them to talk, even about the weather and things like that.

With my daughter, I noticed that she was becoming very tearful and seemed to be stressing out over everything. She kept saying, "I'm not doing well enough." Reassuring her seemed to make no difference. I didn't identify it as depression straight away. I don't think I would have actually used the word 'depression', I would have described it as a 'breakdown'. Then it got to the point where she was crying so much she couldn't go anywhere, and then she started talking about suicide. I knew I had to get help and couldn't manage on my own.

As I began to realise how serious things were, a whole lot of things started running through my mind. My first marriage was violent, so I left. I was then a solo mother and brought the children up on my own, so I immediately thought that it was because of that, because of something that I had done.

Another thing that was in the forefront of my mind was the stigma and the feeling that I was going to be blamed by other people. Further down the track I really had to come to grips with the fact that it wasn't my fault. I had to work through the fact that I did my best as a mother and it wasn't my fault, it was a set of circumstances.

I remember being so concerned about this stigma that I didn't actually tell my family until my daughter was well enough to cope with them. I just felt that I couldn't cope with the possible ridicule. I knew my family would look for a point of blame. That blame label had to hang around somebody's neck, because that is how they perceive mental illness. I was so busy struggling with my daughter and looking after her younger brother, I couldn't bear the thought of somebody blaming me for her being sick.

It was a difficult thing to hide, as I had to take her out of school. By then I had involved a counsellor and the family doctor, who prescribed medication. I think that was when we first started talking about 'depression' *per se*. The doctor had made it clear that we were going to try treating her with antidepressants, and that if she didn't get well, she would have to go to hospital.

I got to the point where I gained strength from just concentrating on getting my daughter well and not worrying about other people. That was all that mattered, and we got there in the end. It was because of my daughter's illness I was able to help my husband with his son.

A Father's Perspective

I haven't had much to do with depression. I always thought of it as a short-term thing. You get depressed about something, you go for a walk in the bush, and then you get over it. That's how I cope with things when I get down. I tend to go off by myself and do something totally different, take on a challenge.

I probably thought that depression was caused by a lack of family support, where there was nobody you could talk to. I know that when my son got sick, I felt that I couldn't talk to anybody. There certainly wasn't anybody outside the family I could go to. When I was a child, we were told to keep all our problems at home – you wouldn't want the neighbours to know about anything.

The age that we were brought up in, everybody dealt with their own problems. My ex-wife's family was the same, and so in our married life we did the same. When you've been brought up to keep your problems to yourself, you do get very good at putting on a mask and hiding things. You don't want to spoil your image by letting people know that you have problems, you just hope they will go away. It was our background, the way we were brought up, and I feel I did the same to my children.

I put Richard's depression down to his earlier life – it wasn't a good family life. My first wife and I didn't communicate, and so we weren't good parents. I have felt very guilty of not giving my son the support I should have as a father. I felt that I didn't stick up for him. All I was interested in at the time was keeping the peace. When he got sick I felt guilty and powerless.

I think nowadays depression is accepted as an illness, rather than a problem within the person themselves. I suppose it's because we're being educated to think about these things differently.

I was very lucky that when my son became depressed I was with my second wife, who had experienced depressive illness before. If I'd been by myself I think I would have gone straight to the doctor, to find out what to do for the best. If he had suggested that committal to a hospital was the only option, I wouldn't have hesitated.

I think it's important to seek medical advice as soon as possible. I would always start with traditional methods, but if everything else failed, I might consider some of these new therapies. I believe that if people hang on too long, they can get into strife because things will be getting worse rather than better.

I remember the doctor being very concerned as to whether or not we would be able to cope with my son if he were to come back and live at home. The doctor wanted one of us to be with him at all times, because of the suicide risk. I relied heavily on my wife at that time. She was the main support, and I used to worry that if the stress got too much for her and she broke down, I wouldn't be able to cope. Now, looking back, I would have done it differently. It has to be a family matter – the whole family – brothers, sisters, everybody.

As it was, we were able to look after Richard at home because we had outside support. If we hadn't been able to do that, we would have had to consider a hospital. We knew that we had someone who could be with him at all times. We had enough people to share the load around, and it wasn't just left with one person, because of course you do have to consider the health of the other people involved as well. If everybody's crashing under the strain, there's no way you're going to cure the problem – it just multiplies, and then you're in a crisis situation.

GWENDOLINE: How did you feel you were able to offer support to Richard throughout his depression?

FATHER: I think the main thing is being prepared to listen – you've got to be understanding and supportive. I think this is easier for women, as they seem to talk about emotional things a lot more than men. It's also a generational thing – people are a lot freer in what they say now than when I was a kid forty years ago. You've got to be prepared to sit there and listen, not say anything – it's just about being there.

I think we all need someone to talk to and solve our problems with, knowing that we can trust that person, that what we have spoken about is safe with them. We need to be able to feel secure. People suffering from depression need to feel that they are in a situation where there are no pressures. They need ongoing support from professionals, for medication or counselling, and they need to know there's always somebody there if they run into a problem.

I hope that my son knows that he is always welcome at home and the door is always open. That if he runs into a problem he doesn't have to be frightened to come home and talk things through. I think this is one of the problems a lot of young people have – they don't know how their parents are going to respond.

MOTHER: I agree with that – you need to be available. You also need to believe in your child and be non-judgemental, and try not to expect too much too soon. I will always remember the day when I came into the room and Richard had done the vacuuming – it was just wonderful that he had got motivated by himself.

I knew there was no point trying to push those things to happen. The 'you've been sick, now get up and get your act together' attitude doesn't help at all, and families need to recognise that. I know from my first experience with my daughter that it takes a long time, and even when the medication's gone and you're a long way down the track, I feel that it is important for your child to feel able to come to you, or go back to a professional adviser. If things aren't going well, she needs to understand that it's a natural progression rather than a relapse.

I know for me it was very helpful being able to pick up the telephone and talk to Richard's therapist and ask, "What should I be doing, am I doing the right thing?" I realise they can't break client confidentiality, but if family members are supporting the person who's ill, they may need help with what to do for the best.

I felt with my daughter that she needed to know that she was free to talk about the things that were important to her, and that may have included her feelings towards me and her father. I do believe that the client must ultimately have privacy in the counselling environment. But the family has to be included at some level.

FROM THOSE WHO KNOW

- **Life must go on**

**You can't be there every moment of the day.
However, especially in the early stages, somebody should be, particularly if there have been suicidal thoughts or attempts. (All suicidal threats need to be taken seriously.)
This responsibility needs to be shared amongst the family.**

- **Being there**

You are helping by merely being present. Go about your normal daily tasks. The knowledge that you are there is really helpful for someone who is depressed. You don't have to feel that you are required to talk all the time or make profound statements.

- **Don't expect anything and you won't be disappointed**

**There's no point in pushing people and trying to make them do things.
Be encouraging but don't place pressure on them.**

- **Being judgemental isn't helpful at the best of times**

They are in a position where they are feeling self-critical and worthless. If they feel it from you, it can only make matters worse.

- **Don't stop talking, especially not to each other**

You will feel frustrated and helpless at times – support each other during these times.

- **The light at the end of the tunnel**

They can't see it, but you still have that ability. Reassurance that things will get better is a wonderful support for someone with depression.

- **You can't fix it on your own!**

Let's Not Forget the Little Ones

The importance of family involvement cannot be emphasised enough. We have spoken about sharing care-giving responsibilities, taking care of each other, going for family therapy sessions. What we haven't covered is how to involve the younger children in the family. They will know that something is wrong, but they won't know what it is. And the longer it goes on, the more confused they will become, and they will also start to feel that they are somehow responsible.

It becomes very difficult for children if it is a parent who is unwell, especially if this involves hospitalisation, or if they have to stay with other family members for long periods of time. This sort of relocation and uncertainty is very stressful for children. They need to have what is happening explained to them.

In her book *How Do We Tell the Kids?*, Pinky McKay describes it beautifully:

Depressed people are very, very sad. They may want to sleep a lot. Sometimes their illness saps all their energy so they can't play with you or talk to you. This doesn't mean they aren't interested in you anymore, or that they don't love you. The doctors will give them treatment to help them get their energy back and they'll learn to be happy again and join in with family activities.

McKay emphasises the importance of support and honesty to help children cope with a family member's illness. Don't forget that children can be quite cruel to each other. In fact, we often hear in their teasing of each other the very rudimentary principles of prejudice with regards mental illness: "Your mother's in a looney bin, she must be nuts. You must be nuts too, nananee nana." Children need to be equipped with ways of explaining things to their friends.

Also inform them that they can choose not to tell people they don't want to talk to. They have a right to say that their mother is unwell and not go any further.

McKay also stresses the importance of using the correct terms to discuss the illness. Explain to them what a psychiatrist does, what sort of doctors they are. They are going to ask questions, and it is important that you answer openly and honestly. You are demystifying the illness for them as well as yourself. Don't forget, depression in a parent predisposes the children to depressive illness later in their own lives. It is an injustice to keep it a secret.

The following suggestions are based on McKay's research on what to expect and how best to deal with questions:

DEPRESSION CAN BE DESCRIBED AS EMOTIONAL PAIN

This is a pain that is much harder to understand than a broken limb because you can't see it. Emphasise, however, that it is an illness, as they may have overheard conversations that describe depression as just having a bad attitude, not caring and being lazy.

CHILDREN NEED TO BE TOLD THE ILLNESS IS NOBODY'S FAULT

They need to know that they didn't cause it, and neither can they make it go away.

DO NOT MAKE FALSE PROMISES

They can be told that the majority of people do get well, but that it takes time for this to happen.

EXPLAIN IT IS NOT CONTAGIOUS LIKE MUMPS OR MEASLES

Depending on the age of the child, they may ask about genetics. Encourage them to read Chapter 1 which will explain the concept of genetic predisposition. Read through this information with them, talking about it as you go, and encouraging them to talk about their feelings, fears and concerns.

Little people's feelings matter too.

CHAPTER 13

When I'm Sixty-Four

WHEN the *Sgt Pepper's Lonely Hearts Club Band* album was released in April of 1967 it hadn't yet occurred to me that there was such an age as sixty-four. There were those of us that were young and then there were old people. Somewhere in the middle were your parents who didn't seem to have an age, only a dedication to cramping your style. Clearly parents had never been teenagers and old people had just always been old. There seemed to be different groups of old people – there were those that gave you a lot of stuff, cooked wonderful food, wanted to kiss and cuddle you – and then there were the grumpy ones, never pleased to see anyone and constantly complaining about noise.

Gazing at the world through the vanity of young adulthood it seemed to make sense that anyone that looked that old and had that many wrinkles, would have to be miserable. That perhaps old age is about misery. When your social life appears to be catching up with your friends at funerals, and talking about the 'good old days', and living with the reality and anxiety of growing old alone. Where retirement becomes a convenient euphemism for redundant, and a generation is left questioning; *"who will still feed me, who will still need me when I'm sixty-four?"*

In a society that appears to place no value on the contribution of its elders, is it surprising that historically the suicide rate for old people has been much higher than for younger people? There is of course significant focus on youth suicide rates, yet the issue of depression in older people has been for the most part unrecognised. Upon reflection, I observe my own oversight when writing the first edition of this book, *Sharing the Load* – I carefully ensured that there was a chapter dedicated to adolescent depression, but it is only now that I find myself five years older and five years closer to 'sixty-four' that I have begun to consider the special nature of late life depression.

Of course our health and mental health dramatically affect and are affected by, aging. However the view that 'depression is not only a normal part of aging but is rampant in old age' is a myth. Margaret Gatz a psychologist specialising in this area came across the following Catch-22: "depression in older adults is exposed to both **overestimation** and **under recognition.**" Confused? Well, what that means is that one assumption concludes that, given all the terrible things associated with aging (multiple problems with health, death of friends and family members, memory loss, wrinkles), of course it's inevitable that they will become depressed. But the concern is, that because being at least a bit depressed is considered a normal part of the aging process, doctors fail to recognise or treat depressive disorder among their older patients. And of course families fall into the same trap.

In the process of writing this chapter I spoke with two highly skilled geriatric psychiatrists, I listened to the wisdom of an old man who had battled depression, and I experienced the loss of my father to Parkinson's, another neurological disorder with depression as its bedfellow. In the pages to follow I will share with you some of the knowledge and insights that I gained and hopefully, by it's completion you will have sufficient knowledge and understanding to recognise the difference between, *'Uncle Bob's just eccentric, old and grumpy all the time'* and *'Uncle Bob could be suffering from depression'* and then along with that knowledge, some guidelines for how to help your loved one.

This issue of not recognising depression in the elderly was one of the first questions I put to Dr Chris Perkins, a colleague of mine and a specialist in mental health and the elderly.

GWENDOLINE: I was surprised to find that the rates of depression and suicide for the elderly was so high; you don't seem to hear about old people committing suicide.

CHRIS: One wonders of course if it is as simple as being overlooked or is it justified as "they're old they may as well commit suicide, it's a philosophical choice, just like euthanasia. I'd want to commit suicide if I looked that old, it's understandable." But in fact most suicide doesn't occur in that way, it's more often as a result of depression, so it can be quite a hidden problem. Then combine this with people, families and doctors saying, "Well you're old, you've got bad hips, you've lost your husband, of course you're depressed what do you expect?"

GWENDOLINE: What about the reaction of the older person themselves, do they recognise what is happening?

CHRIS: The elderly now are the age group that have been through the war and great economic hardship, and it's important to keep a 'stiff upper lip' – admitting to depression is difficult and often they won't recognise it. They are more comfortable with complaining about physical symptoms and this focus will often mask the depression. It is also the case that people of different ethnic groups may speak of depressive symptoms using different terminology.

The other way depression can present in older people, is with confusion and memory loss. These are both symptoms of depression but can look like a dementia and hence, are often misdiagnosed. People just think they are getting old and a bit demented or see it as the early signs of Alzheimers.

The prevalence of physical illness does leave people more vulnerable to depression at any age, and with age does come an increase in health problems. There is, of course, a sense of loss associated with disabilities that inhibit movement and independence. These factors all contribute. Certainly depression is more common in residential care, eg. rest homes, private hospitals (with some studies estimating 30-40%).

GWENDOLINE: With all of these physical possibilities and presentations being part of getting older, how can the family recognise depression in their loved one?

CHRIS: Even if people are complaining of terrible stomach discomfort or aches and pains, the symptoms of depression can still be identified. It's just a matter of asking the right questions and being specific. They'll tell you about the symptoms even if they ascribe them to something else. It is unusual for someone over the age of 65 to be experiencing their first episode, hence you might suspect there is another condition present. For instance, it is often difficult to tell the difference between dementia and depression, as they can look the same at the onset. In both cases the person slows down, there is a loss of enjoyment, they can't concentrate, they don't remember.

Depression can also be common in the early stages of dementia and the other neurological disorders such as Parkinson's, so thorough assessments are important. Depression is also very common after a stroke, but even if the depression is secondary to another condition it's important that it is treated anyway – it's not hopeless, just because people are old and have multiple health problems.

Some Things to Look Out For

1. Losing interest in activities and interests.

2. Preferring to stay at home rather than go out and do new things

3. Appear to be worried/anxious that something bad might happen to them.

4. Not happy and lacking in energy.

5. Pessimistic about the future

6. Complaining of being bored (nothing to look forward to).

7. Has sad or depressed mood, has wished to be dead anytime during the past month.

6. Not eating or drinking

Along With Some Questions You Can Ask

1. **Are you still basically satisfied with your life?**
2. **Do you often feel helpless, that your life is empty?**
3. **Are you bothered about thoughts that you cannot get out of your head?**
4. **Would you say you were in a good mood most of the time?**
5. **Do you feel you have more problems with memory than most?**
6. **Do you feel worthless and that your situation is hopeless?**
7. **Do you think most people are better off than you are?**
8. **Do you get upset over little things and feel like crying?**
9. **Do you have trouble concentrating and feel like crying?**
10. **Do you find it difficult to get motivated and prefer to avoid social situations?**

The questions above are taken from clinical assessment tools for the diagnosis of geriatric depression. Take it from the words of experience these are difficult questions to ask, especially if it is your mother or father you are worried about. It is not easy to face the possibility that your parent or loved one wants to end their life, but it is better that you know and can begin a process of getting treatment.

GWENDOLINE. It would seem that a number of the questions on that list could equally apply to a grief reaction. How can families know the difference?

CHRIS: If the grief reaction goes on for months, the family will actually look back and say, "*She used to be much more outgoing and she used to enjoy the grandchildren more.*" "*He's more irritable and more isolated and he doesn't want to go to his clubs anymore.*" These are all tell-tale signs and fairly reliable ones at that.

Often when the death of a spouse is involved, there are studies that show the vulnerability of the remaining spouse and the subsequently high death rate. Older men are a higher suicide risk. This generation of men are often less skilled at accessing support and older men have often been dependent on their wives for things like social contact, cooking, ironing, cleaning – life-skills in other words. So as the family, you have to become very aware of the possibility of depression developing. Look out for things like changes in sleep patterns, look for changes in behaviour.

Speaking with Dr. Gavin Pilkington, another colleague of mine, he came up with these thoughts on:

What Else You Can Do

GAVIN: Grief counselling is an option but often this generation are reluctant to involve themselves with things to do with 'mental' health. If they are sitting on that borderline of grief and depression, encouraging them to participate in family activities can have some value. However, if they have crossed the line and the grief has become depression, you often have to give them a helping hand through the use of medication.

GWENDOLINE: How can a family instigate going to a doctor and possibly taking a pill, when this older group do tend to be a lot more conservative when talking about emotions and participating in personal disclosure?

GAVIN: My experience is that families are incredibly different and that they will find the way that feels most comfortable. Often the family will have to go to the doctor themselves and encourage the parent/older relative along with them.

GWENDOLINE: When it comes to the use of medications are there any types of medications that are preferable for the elderly and are there things to look out for?

GAVIN: What dictates the choice of medications is most often to do with the presence of other possible medical/surgical conditions that older people may have. However, these decisions are not medically difficult. For instance, we would use SSRI'S (Selective Serotonin Reuptake Inhibitors, see page 39): they're heart friendly, don't alter blood pressure a great deal, they don't compromise cognition (thinking processes) and they compromise reaction time a lot less, so they probably are now the first choice for older people. They are also safer, particularly if there is any indication of suicidal thinking. By that I mean they are not as dangerous with overdose.

(i) You will get side effects as you do with other medications and they need to be monitored.
(ii) You do need to watch for agitation.
(iii) A drop in sodium levels needs to be checked for in the first eight weeks (monitored most likely by your family doctor).

Apart from medication there are other things you can do to be helpful. Here are a few:

Other Approaches

1. EDUCATION ABOUT DEPRESSION

Being educated is very important: understanding depression and what their loved one may be experiencing. Gather as much information as you can, but from reputable sources. Have resources recommended from those that are educated and informed. Be wary of the internet – there is a lot of very unhelpful, biased information available. Look for sites recommended by your doctor and/or government agencies.

2. COGNITIVE THERAPY

Cognitive therapy makes an important contribution in this area by examining the themes of negative thought people have about themselves, the world and the future. This form of negative thinking can be a result of the depression, and also serves in maintaining the depression. For instance, "I'm not going to take on any new hobbies, what's the point? I'm a burden to my family, they would be better off if I was dead." Cognitive therapists work with the understanding that these thoughts can be worked with and adjusted to improve, rather than depress mood. They also place emphasis on behaviour and how inactivity and social isolation can influence, and reinforce depression.

Families through involvement with the cognitive therapist can learn to distinguish between what behaviour and thinking are controlling, and what the depression is controlling. The more informed families can be, the more they are able to support 'wellness' and minimise the effects of the depression, but NOT in a 'pull yourself together' kind of way.

(For more information about Cognitive Therapy, see page 50 and the suggested reading list, p.155)

3. REASSURANCE

This is particularly important when dealing with the themes of – 'being a burden, not being wanted, getting in the way, placing financial strain, better off dead'. This thinking can be very much part of the depression but it is also very common with older people. The link is back to the very basic need for security. Old age is unpredictable, people begin to worry about *"What will happen to me if I have another stroke or a heart attack? What will happen to me if I have no money? Where will I go? Who will be there for me?"* These are very real concerns and will come through as a part of depressive thinking. We also see these themes appear in patients with dementia.

The older person will often find it difficult to distinguish between what is factual and real in their environment and what is a reflection of their feelings about what they are experiencing. Therapists and psychologists can be very helpful in assisting the family to find a way to talk about these issues with their loved one during the recovery phase.

4. GRIEF COUNSELLING

There are significant themes of loss associated with old age; health, death of friends, financial insecurity, loss of a spouse. Therapy focusing on the stages of grief and normalising the process can also contribute a great deal.

5. KEEP THEM OCCUPIED

Keeping people occupied is far more useful than allowing them to sit and dwell on how bad they feel, going over and over things in their head, endlessly worrying. This of course is the same for all age groups but especially important with older people as they can be more isolated, have lost their licence to drive, and hence be unable to keep in contact with friends through independent means.

I want to complete this chapter by introducing you in writing to a wonderful man. Some cultures would simply refer to him, and revere him as an 'Elder'. He was willing to share with me these insights, from his wisdom and through the pain of his own experience of depression. He remains nameless because his sadness could belong to your father and mine.

"When an old man is depressed the first thing to do is be kind to him"

"After my wife died I was quite happy but I was missing her inside and that used to get me down. My family wanted me to move in with them, but that meant I had to dismantle my libraries and all my personal surroundings, I started to feel that I had no home and then I started to feel very sad. My younger brother died and I went home to Fiji for the funeral – there was more unhappiness.

"When I returned to my son's house it had been broken into, and then along with the sadness I then started to feel scared and frightened that the thieves would return. One day after breakfast I went and lay down on my bed and thought about these things over and over again. I worried that the thieves would come and steal everything and we would be homeless. I started to worry about what I would do, and I came to the conclusion that this life is useless, that the longer I hang onto life the more trouble there will be. I started to have strange thoughts and experiences, my head was swinging and things were moving and I would feel wobbly and could not walk properly."

GWENDOLINE: It sounded as though you had started to become quite paranoid and frightened. That you were starting to have some suicidal thoughts, and perhaps the beginnings of delusions or hallucinations.

"YES, and I said to my son that there was something wrong and I needed to see a doctor. The doctor said to me, "Sometimes you get worried and there's no cure for that, there is no medication, you just need some time to yourself."

I went home but I got more and more depressed and paranoid about things, especially to do with my pension and money and what I should be doing with tax payments. I went to the doctor again and got some sleeping pills and because they weren't helping me I took all of them. I knew that I was taking an overdose. I ended up in hospital was treated with anti-depressants and some ECT (electro-convulsive therapy see page 44)

They were very kind to me in the hospital and with the treatment I started to take an interest in life again. I started socializing through social groups organized through the hospital and through a community church group. It took a while to get my confidence back, but I have started to regain my independence."

GWENDOLINE: It must have been a great shock for your family when you ended up in hospital. How did they manage and what did they do that was most helpful for you?

"MY son started to take a great interest to make sure that I was OK, but he would do things in a certain way so that I would not necessarily feel I was being watched. He organized for me to join a library so I had books available to read and would meet other people. My son's wife works with old people and she was very kind to me and made sure I was eating and taking care of myself.

"I thought I was such a burden on my family, I felt like I was a burden and that I wasn't doing anything and that I was of no use to people. That's what I put in my suicide note, they should have my money and make good use of it, I did a foolish thing and will never do that again."

GWENDOLINE: Do you think it's a true statement that often depression in older people does not get noticed until, as with you they become suicidal and make a desperate cry for help?

"AS a person gets old and can do less, the children are busy with their own work and their own lives. I would sit and watch and feel depressed and all I could think was, I should be busy too, but that depressed feeling is there all the time. You don't feel that you can communicate what it is and you also worry that if you expressed how bad you felt you might have to go to a home or be put somewhere and that would be worse.

People who are old today, when they were young they contributed and as they grow old society must do something to look after them, whether their children look after them or not. Why should elderly people be left to feel that they have been put off, discarded?

What I need as an old man, and I think it's the same for an old lady, is just to be noticed. Younger people are always so busy and sometimes make you feel like an intrusion if you ask them for things, or to pay attention to something you have done, when you get that feeling, that's very sad.

When an old man is depressed the very first thing they should do is be kind to him and try to fulfil his needs – just the little things leave you feeling loved and cared for and happier."

Something Especially For You

I have spoken before in this book about the secret burden of care. A secret because the family and the loved ones 'shouldn't' be feeling resentful about caring for someone you love. 'Should' is a widely used word but not that helpful apart from the purposes of evoking guilt. Taking care of a loved one particularly, if there are dual conditions, such as dementia or physical illness along with the depression, is difficult. It is both painful and exhausting. You are confronted with the vulnerability of someone you may have looked up to all your life, which also raises your own sense of mortality and fragility. So it is hard and…

REMEMBER

Don't try to do everything on your own – network into as many support systems and professional resources as possible. There are many facilities that can offer 'respite' care when needed.

You are allowed to feel frustrated at times – it doesn't mean you have stopped loving them.

People do get tired of living and that's healthy, but old age is not about being preoccupied with death – that's depression.

CHAPTER 14

You've Got a Friend

IT TAKES a lot of tolerance, love and understanding to support a depressed friend. There needs to be a very strong commitment to the friendship for it to survive the long months ahead. There will be times when you feel that nothing you are doing is in the slightest bit helpful, that nothing you say seems to be making a difference. You're trying so hard to be understanding and yet at times you don't feel as if you are getting through. You question whether what you are doing is for the best. Are you doing the right thing when you listen to them talk about how bad they are feeling? Or should you just tell them to snap out of it? Should you take them away for the weekend and invite lots of your mutual friends? Should you throw a party? Should you be doing more, should you be doing less, or should you be doing something completely different? It's not easy.

When people are depressed, one of their biggest fears is that they will lose their friends because they have "become so boring and are such a burden". From one who knows, the best thing you can do is to be yourself and just be there. Upon saying that, there are other quite practical things that you can do, which can not only contribute to your friend's recovery but also enable the family to cope a little better.

The following are excerpts from conversations I had with a few of my dear friends, who found their own ways of helping me through what was to be along and cold journey back to health. I feel confident that you will find something amongst these words of wisdom and kindness that will help you comfort your very dear friend. For they are suffering, and they do need you, even if sometimes they try and tell you they don't.

A Few Tips on How to Care (from those who did)

LINDA: My understanding of depression is that there are two levels – one is when people talk about feeling depressed and then there's depressive illness. I would treat a friend who was depressed like any friend with an illness. I don't think of it as an attitude.

I also think it's important to be involved with the family and other friends. I see it as providing a safety net. If other people know that things aren't right, they can keep an eye on the person. This would apply in the work environment, where a person's functioning would be greatly impaired by depression.

I'm a great believer in offering very practical support such as making food and trying to provide some creature comforts, like making sure the person stays in bed if that's what is needed – the real 'Jewish Momma' approach that chicken soup cures most things, particularly if it's served with love. It's not just a question of force-feeding someone.

GWENDOLINE: It was very important for me to feel that there was no pressure to eat all the food on the plate. It always made me feel good when Linda would say little things like, "Just eat what you can." For some people, having anything to do with food is very difficult when depressed. Often people don't eat at all if they are on their own. Just being with friends enables them to relax long enough to digest the food.

We would also go walking, and I would know that if I needed to talk about how bad I was feeling, I could. I didn't expect answers. You shouldn't expect yourself to come up with answers – you're there as a presence, as a comfort, just to listen. It helps.

RAINE: I feel that it is important to be supportive and reassuring. Depression seems to take away people's ability to cope. They are no longer able to cope with life's everyday setbacks without being totally flattened. Things that would normally be so easy, that were done without thinking, become difficult and seem insurmountable.

I tried to offer the reassurance that getting well takes time, that you have to face one day at a time and put one foot in front of the other. If you have a bad day, that's all it is, a bad day, and the next day you get up and start again. I also feel that it is important to see the smallest accomplishment as being an important achievement, and play down the setbacks, so that the focus isn't on how bad things are, which collapses the sense of progress.

Working alongside the family is necessary. Even though you don't want to interfere with what the family is doing, I feel it is important to have some information about what is happening. The more friends who know, the more they can be there to share the burden. Friends are able to be there and give the family a break, stay the night if needed.

Most of all, I think it's making yourself available, just being there to talk through things. I tend to see getting well as a process, and you need to talk your way through it.

GWENDOLINE: Depressed people do a lot of things that make life hard. They doubt themselves, they expect too much, they only ever see what they have done wrong, never what they have achieved. If you, like my friend, have that wonderful gift of patience, use it to take them through their achievements, and remind them of their progress, no matter how small. Reassure them that things will get better, that they are getting better, but it won't happen overnight.

DONNA: I used to think that being depressed was just being a bit low, feeling weepy and unable to control your emotions, and that the mood passes and you just snap out of it. I wasn't sure what to do at first. The worst part for me, as a friend was not knowing what was going on and what to do.

I felt that it was important to try and bring things back to normality in some way – in a subtle way, like having close friends at home, rather than socialising amongst strangers, and to try to encourage a process of slowly re-emerging.

GWENDOLINE: And it is a slow process. Being thrown into large social gatherings too soon is very daunting and unsettling. Starting to have friends over to my home was a very important step forward. It placed me in a position of having to cook a meal, which was a major task, but, when complete, it was something that could be seen as an achievement and it helped to rebuild my confidence.

What you have to realise is that for your friend, everything has slowed down, everything is magnified, small things seem large, perceptions are distorted by the illness. You will be surprised how important the smallest contributions are – they can make such a difference.

KATHRYN: I don't know enough about depression or psychiatric illness to jump to the conclusion that someone is unwell. I'd probably go through a list of things to explain changes in behaviour before I would think of that. It's almost as though, if it's a friend, you don't want it to be a mental illness. I would have to say that it was an acute learning curve for me. I've been able to see more things in hindsight.

Being tolerant was important. Trying to work in with the family, but without encroaching on privacy, was another thing. With your own family you know you can take things further, you can insist on being involved. It's almost as though how much you become involved is a selfish decision. It depends on how much it affects you. If it affects you a lot, you want things to be dealt with very quickly and want more say about what happens with professional intervention and all other aspects of the situation.

GWENDOLINE: What Kathryn is saying is very true. How much you are involved and how much you have to offer is very much related to the nature of the relationship. Because someone you know is depressed, you don't immediately have to rush in and be there at the front line; you can be there in the way you always have been. Perhaps a little more, but only if that feels right. Don't offer help because you feel obliged – it won't work for either of you. Sending flowers and saying, you care may be just what the doctor ordered.

Just remember: Being there is the most important thing of all!

AUTHOR'S NOTE

Since I wrote the first edition, *Sharing the Load*, almost six years have passed. In that time I am six years further away from the experience of my own illness. I have taken much joy from seeing many people benefit from reading this book and passing it on to others – even if I do miss out on the royalties. I have worked with many, many more people suffering from depression and listened to the shared experiences of their families. I have also in that time lost my father to Parkinson's disease. During that time I couldn't help but selfishly anticipate and fear a further episode of my own illness. But most of all I observed another debilitating 'psychoneurological disorder' take a life and shatter a family.

Through my eyes as a clinician, I saw the same themes: misunderstanding, lack of resource, ignorance and perhaps stigma – evidenced in the difference in palliative care from somatic conditions, such as cancer – as I have so frequently witnessed as part of the course of depressive and other psychiatric disorders. Somewhere ingrained in our psyches, in our society, within our health systems and within our legislative systems, is the belief that somehow psychic pain is not as valid or as real as physical pain.

If it takes another ten books or the rest of my career, whatever comes first, I will continue to fight for the validation and the right to adequate treatment, for the individuals and their families, dealing with "**suffering of the mind**".

GLOSSARY

The following definitions are explanations of diagnostic terms that I have used in the text.

Bipolar Disorder

This term is more commonly known as 'manic depression'. The most useful way to understand the disorder is to think of the two 'polar opposites' of mood: depression (feeling really down) and mania (feeling very high and elevated). Our normal mood variation is between feeling happy and cheerful to at times feeling sad and despondent. As we move along the continuum these fluctuations become more extreme.

Hypomania

This is a term used by psychiatrists to describe a mild form of mania. Mild refers to the fact that although it is distressful, the sufferer can more often than not be managed outside of hospital.

Lithium

This is a medication used to stabilise mood. Lithium was first renowned for its anti-manic properties. Since its discovery it has been used to prevent the recurrence of mania and depression and to treat acute episodes of mania as well as treatment-resistant depression. As a mood stabiliser it is a maintenance medication and, once prescribed, a person can expect to take it for up to years at a time.

SELECTED READING

BRADLEY, D. *The Hyperventilation Syndrome* (Tandem Books, 1994)

BURNS, D. *Feeling Good* (Avon Books, 1992)

COPELAND, M.E. *The Depression Workbook* (New Harbinger Publications, 1992)

CYTRYN, L and McKNEW, D. *Growing Up Sad: Childhood Depression and its Treatment* (W.W. Norton & Company, 1998)

DAVIS, M., ESHELMAN E. and McKAY, M. *The Relaxation and Stress Reduction Workbook* (New Harbinger Publications, 1995)

FASSLER, D.G. and DUMAS, L.S. *Help Me I'm Sad: Recognising, Treating and Preventing Childhood and Adolescent Depression* (Penguin Books, 1997)

McKAY, P. *How Do We Tell the Kids?* (Prentice Hall, 1995)

MILLIGAN, S. and CLARE, A. *Depression and How to Survive it* (Arrow, 1994)

PENNEBAKER, J.W. *Opening Up: The Healing Power of Confiding in Others* (W. Morrow, 1990)

PETRIE, BOOTH AND DAVISON, 'Repression, Disclosure and Immune Function', Pennebaker, J.W. (ed.) *Emotion, Disclosure and Health* American Psychological Association, 1995

QUALLS, S.H. AND ABELES, N (ed) *Psychology and the aging Revolution* (American Psychological Association, 2000)

SELIGMAN, M. *What You Can Change and What You Can't* (Random House, 1994)

SKYNNER, R. AND CLEESE, J. *Families and How to Survive Them* (Methuen, 1983)

Some Helpful Websites

The internet has been both a gift and a curse when it comes to the provision of information on depression. There are vast and ever-increasing numbers of sites available on the topic. However, not all of these are helpful. Here are some of my favourites, because they come from credible and reliable sources.

www.mentalhealthfoundation.co.nz
www.beyondblue.com.au
www.DepNet.com.au
www.aacap.org
www.nimh.nih.gov
www.mind.org.uk
www.wfmh.org/links.html
www.nami.org
and
www.depressionexplained.com

NOTES